You Can Make
Wire & Bead Jewelry

Patricia DeMarco

Schiffer Publishing Ltd

4880 Lower Valley Road   Atglen, Pennsylvania 19310

 Contents

Other Schiffer Books on Related Subjects:
Designing Jewelry: Brooches, Bracelets, Necklaces &
Accessories, Maurice P. Galli, Dominique Riviere, & Fanfan Li.
Beaded Fantasies: Beads & Strings Jewelry, Ani Afshar

Designed by Mark David Bowyer
Type set in Isadora / Humanist521 BT

ISBN: 978-0-7643-2729-2
Printed in China

Published by Schiffer Publishing Ltd.
4880 Lower Valley Road
Atglen, PA 19310
Phone: (610) 593-1777; Fax: (610) 593-2002
E-mail: Info@schifferbooks.com

For the largest selection of fine reference books on this and related subjects, please visit our web site at
www.schifferbooks.com
We are always looking for people to write books on new and related subjects. If you have an idea for a book please contact us at the above address.

This book may be purchased from the publisher.
Include $3.95 for shipping.
Please try your bookstore first.
You may write for a free catalog.

In Europe, Schiffer books are distributed by
Bushwood Books
6 Marksbury Ave.
Kew Gardens
Surrey TW9 4JF England
Phone: 44 (0) 20 8392-8585; Fax: 44 (0) 20 8392-9876
E-mail: info@bushwoodbooks.co.uk
Website: www.bushwoodbooks.co.uk
Free postage in the U.K., Europe; air mail at cost.

Dedication

I dedicate this book first and foremost to my husband, Guy, for his love, support, and encouragement. He has provided assistance with the technical aspects, such as buying supplies and setting up the scanner and printer, and his many trips to the store for paper, discs, and other supplies.

Also, to my family, particularly the women in the family, for loving me and wearing my jewelry, which is truly a sign of respect for my creations: my daughter Lisa, my sister Vicki, step-daughter Gina, and granddaughters Tiana, Victoria, Amanda, and Elyssa. Victoria allowed me to do a jewelry-making lesson with her Girl Scout troop.

Also, to Doctor James Warwick and his beloved Lil. He was my dearest friend, mentor in graduate school, and teacher of a graduate jewelry class, where I first started to make jewelry. He was my inspiration to explore anything and everything that pertained to creating.

Finally, to the many women who have complimented me on the jewelry that I was wearing and become close friends, and therefore recipients of my jewelry. They believed that they also could explore their own creativity.

1. Introduction

The desire to create and seek different avenues to travel in order to express my own creativity has been a journey since I was old enough to hold a paint brush in my hand and apply watercolor to the page. My introduction to jewelry making was a graduate course at Queen's College, which I thoroughly enjoyed. My busy life, at that time, and the cost of the tools and equipment needed for the type of jewelry that I did in school, involving soldering and cutting silver, almost kept me from continuing. Two important elements of the jewelry-making in this book address the use of time and the affordability of materials.

My introduction to making jewelry began with finding, in a closet at Nassau Community College, kits with jewelry-making tools. I took the kit, experimented, and loved working with wire, pliers, various other tools, and beads to create my own jewelry.

At the time, I was teaching a Basic Crafts class, so the following semester I introduced what I learned that summer. The new concepts for jewelry making were a hit with most of the students.

Over the years, I have continued to find time to create jewelry, which I have never sold. I either wear my creations or give them away as a gift. Often, I have been asked if I would form a class and teach jewelry making. This book is my class.

The art of jewelry making is fun, affordable, and possible to do for anyone who has a desire to create jewelry that expresses their own personality and style. Today's style is very unique and individual.

What I love about the process of jewelry making is that the materials needed are not expensive and are readily available. The space to create is as minimal as a flat surface, and the time to create can be broken up into small bits of time, so that it can be an on-going process that allows you to finish. Affordability is another benefit. I often buy what I like a little at a time, and therefore have an on-going stash of beads and wire to work with. Some of the tools can be hand-made.

Hopefully, I will convince you, the readers, to take the time to experiment with making jewelry and grow, as I did, to love the process and to share with others the finished pieces.

2. Elements and Principles of Design

To understand the rules that I follow when creating a piece of jewelry, the reader needs to know and understand the elements and principles of design. There are examples and directions for many pieces of jewelry that I hope you enjoy creating, but hopefully you will go beyond these examples and create your own designs.

Color

My starting point for design is usually color. When I am looking at an array of beads I am drawn to certain colors, which are probably the same colors that I am attracted to when I buy clothing. Your choice of color is very important, because no one likes to complete something that they don't like from the beginning. The assortment of bead colors today is vast. Don't hesitate to change the color of a design in this book to a color that you like and that would make the jewelry your own individual approach to design.

Shapes & Sizes

Beads don't just come in different colors, they also come in different shapes and sizes. Beads range in size from 2mm to 14mm. Unlike wire, the smaller the number means the smaller the bead. Again, you as an individual will be attracted to certain shapes and sizes. Learning to balance the shapes and sizes when you are designing jewelry is very important. It is easy to do symmetrical balance, where one side is the same as the other. Asymmetrical balance, where the sides aren't the same, can still look balanced.

Two groups of beads that aren't the same can take up the same amount of space and length, which makes them look balanced. Also, two single beads of the same size but different design can look balanced. You will see in a few of the designs that each unit is different, but in the final design they look balanced and create a unified piece of jewelry.

The beads can be large, or small, or a combination of large and small. The size you choose will certainly give a different feel to the jewelry.

Color Variety

Once you have picked the colors you love, you may ask, "How do I pick a variety of colors?" One way is to stay *monochromatic* and pick different values and shades of the same color. Another consideration is to choose *analogous* colors, such as colors that are next to each other on the color wheel: yellow, yellow orange, orange, red orange, red, red, purple, blue purple, blue, blue green, green, yellow green, and back to yellow.

Another choice is to use *complimentary* colors, which are opposite on the color wheel: red and green, blue and orange, or purple and yellow. The *warm colors* are yellow to red-purple, and the *cool colors* are blue-purple to yellow-green.

Hole Size

When buying beads, make sure the opening in the bead corresponds to the width of the wire you want to use. Sometimes large beads can have a small opening and small beads can have a large opening. A good tool to have is a *bead reamer*, which allows you to widen a bead's hole opening by filing away some of the inside of the bead. The bead opening must be compatible with the width of the wire you will use.

Texture

Along with a bead's color, shape, and size, you will need to consider its texture. A bead can be glossy or matte (dull), translucent (see through), or opaque (cannot see through), smooth or rough, and heavy or light, in appearance as well as in actual weight.

Space

A key element of design is space. How close or far apart are the beads? I particularly like the beads to be able to, as I say, breathe. I like them to be noticed along with the wire that attaches the beads and to be balanced, with all elements being of equal importance.

The principles of design play an important role in the appearance of your finished jewelry. Repetition, Unity, Contrast and Movement in various combinations is the basis of the art of designing jewelry. Will each of the elements be the same in *repetition*, or different in complete *contrast*? Repetition creates unity and contrast creates excitement. Repetition and contrast can work together to create a dynamic piece of jewelry.

Size

The size of the jewelry also determines the design of the jewelry. A short choker necklace is quite different than a 20-inch long necklace.

3. Materials

Now that you have selected your beads, you need to get the materials and tools you will need to connect the beads, based on the designs shown in this book or on your own unique designs. All of the beads in this book are strung on wire, and the individual units of beads are connected by wire, so I will start with wire.

Wire

Wire is annealed, or softened, by heating. Annealed wire will bend and twist without breaking, and make it possible for you to design with the wire. The package of wire should say *annealed* or *okay for jewelry making*.

Wire comes in different gauges, which means the width of the wire. The higher the number, the thinner the wire (unlike bead sizes, as previously mentioned). In my jewelry making, I usually use 20 gauge and 22 gauge wire. In some of the designs in this book it is possible to substitute 18 gauge wires. I have used wire with 18, 20, 22, and 24 gauge wires.

There are many different kinds of wire. The least expensive wire is *copper*, which is great to use for experimentation and it can be used for finished jewelry, as shown in this book. *Silver* wire can be sterling silver, the most expensive of the silver wires but still affordable. Sterling wire creates the most beautiful look. *Non-tarnishing silver* wire, which is a little cheaper, still creates a fine piece of jewelry. Wire just *marked silver* will darken with time. *Gold* wire that is pure gold is very expensive, but the *gold filled* wire is more affordable and very attractive.

Wire comes in different styles, *round* or *square*. In most cases, I use round wire. There are a few examples here of square wire. The wires described in the designs of this book are certainly very limited in styles compared to the many varieties of wire on the market.

Tools

The most important tool is a pair of pliers. There are three different pliers that I use which are the round nose pliers, flat nose pliers, and needle nose pliers. Chain nose pliers are nice to have. In all cases the jaws should be smooth so that the wire doesn't get scratched. I buy moderately priced pliers and they work fine. Wire cutters are very necessary and here I would not buy the cheapest but would go toward the more expensive. It is important that the wire is cut sharply and quickly so that there are smooth cuts. A small file is necessary to smooth out the rough edges (burrs).

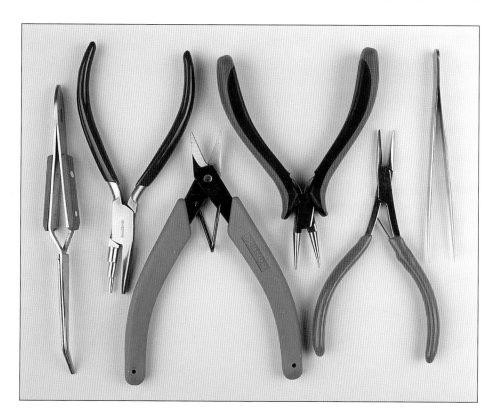

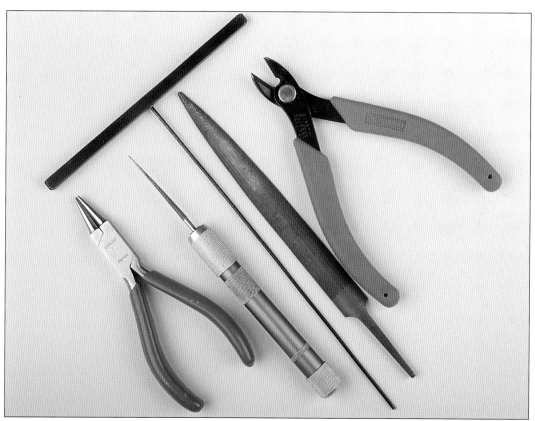

Jig

Repetitive designs are usually made on a jig, to guarantee that the repeat is exact. Jigs are fun to work with and can be either store bought or home made. I have two jigs. The first jig is metal and the second jig is plastic. The width of the jig determines the width that the final jig piece can be. The length is usually not an issue.

When working with a jig wind the first circle with round nose pliers in two steps. Measure 3/8th inch from the end of the wire and bend the end back at a right angle. Place the round nose pliers at the end of the wire and wind half way around. Reposition the pliers at the end and continue to twist until the circle is made. Place this circle on the first peg of the jig. Continue to wind around the pegs in the order shown. End with a tight wind around the last peg and cut off any excess wire. A metal jig I find is easier to work with because you can get a tighter wind since the metal has enough resistance for the pull of the wire to be tight but a plastic jig is great when working with a thinner gauge wire so buy both kinds of jigs.

A difficult part of making pieces on the jig occurs when you have to duplicate the piece a few times. You really want all the pieces to look identical. Don't hesitate to eliminate any pieces that don't look identical and start again to duplicate the original piece. I never throw away any jig-made pieces. You might find use for them in another piece of jewelry. I duplicate a piece for the other side of a necklace or pair of earrings by turning the original piece over and use that piece as my model for placement of wire and pegs on the jig.

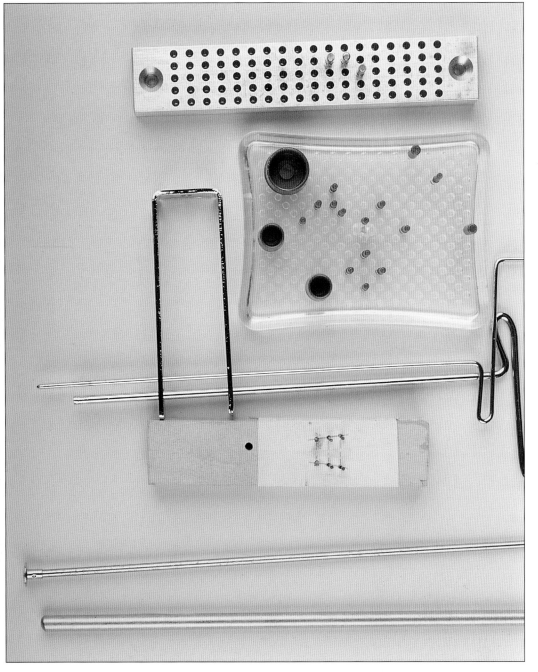

When I start a piece on the jig, I work from the entire spool or wrapped winding of wire. I pull away what I approximate the length will be without cutting the wire. It is hard to give the exact lengths because every body has a different tension or pull on the jig. It is just like making a sample crochet or knitting piece to judge the gauge needed to make the proper length. The only time I have to cut before the end is when I am placing a bead on the wire. Here I judge how much wire I need to wind around the last peg and always over estimate so I'm not caught short.

Jig pieces are an interesting way to give length to a piece of jewelry, separate the distance between beads, hold a bead and provide the drop for a pendant. Most of the jig pieces in the book are original designs that happened by playing with different arrangements of pegs. Use copper or any other inexpensive wire to do your own experimentation. Like any creative adventure it is always beneficial to do many possible approaches or solutions for design.

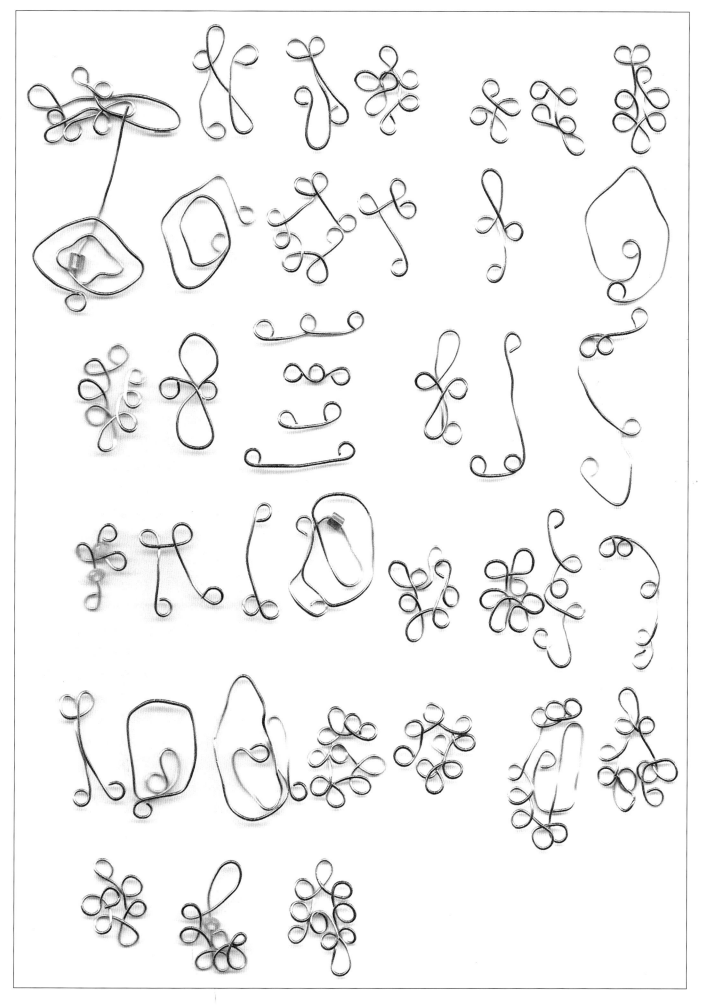

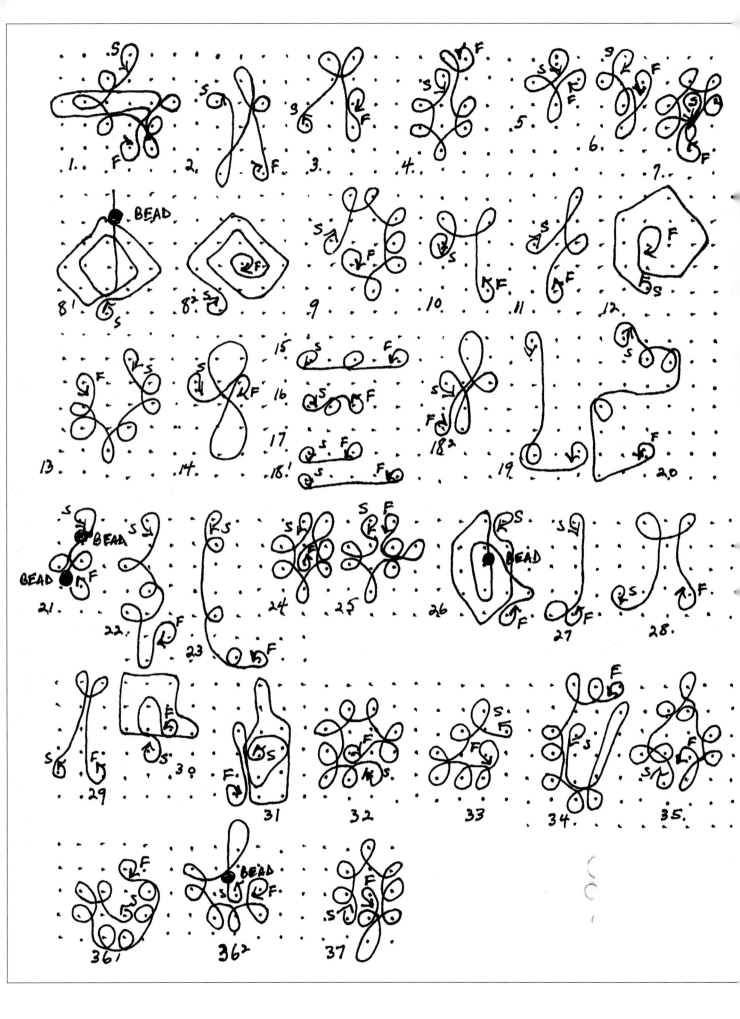

Rings

Jump rings, which are the rings used to attach pieces together, can be store-bought. I have never bought rings and chose to make my own. They are simple to make and if made from the wire that holds the units of beads there is a guarantee of compatibility. Sometimes I use two different sizes of rings in one piece of jewelry.

The size of the jump ring is determined by the size of the *mandrel* (the tool that the wire is being wound around). I use a metal knitting needle as a mandrel and have bought different tools that allow you to wrap wire. When the wire has been properly wrapped, with each piece lying parallel to the adjacent piece, and taken off the mandrel, individual rings are cut from the unit. There should be no space between the wraps.

It is necessary to use two flat-nose pliers to open and close the rings so that the original shape doesn't get lost in the bending. Only open one end as far as is needed, by holding each end of the circle and gently pushing one side back or forward. You are separating the ring sideways at the cut. Close the space by bringing the ends toward the middle a little bit past the center. Move both ends back and forth until the wire clicks closed. Tighten the closing by placing the flat nose pliers across the closing and press.

Discard any rings that you are unhappy with, in the closing or the shape. The connectors are as important to the design as is any other part of the jewelry-making process.

Findings

The pieces used to connect or hold the beads together along with the wire are the *findings*. Clasps to close the necklace or bracelet, ear wires and posts, pin backings, head pins and eye pins are used to hold beads or connect beads. I usually make the clasps for a necklace. Cut a piece of wire from 3 ½ inches to 4 inches. Fold back over round nose pliers a little more than half of the wire. Pinch together with a flat nose pliers starting from the center toward the end and have the longer piece of wire facing you. Hold the two folded wires together at the end with a round nose pliers and fold the single wire up and then around in two steps.

Wind the single wire around the double wire at least three times. Cut off the excess wire. Always file the cut ends so that they are smooth.

When I first began to work with wire it felt awkward; now it is a way of life. If I am away from jewelry making for a long time, I make sure in my busy schedule that I find time to create something new. There is always a gift to give.

Bead Units

When creating a bead unit, the method that you use depends on the thickness of the wire. First, the wire is bent back at a right angle for 3/8 of an inch. For 20 gauge or thicker wire, make a circle in two steps by placing the pliers at the end of the wire and twist half way up. Reposition the pliers and continue to twist until the circle is closed. One side can twist up and the other side can twist down. In jewelry making, you are working with the laws of physics so the piece of jewelry lies correctly on your body and doesn't twist the wrong way.

When working with 22 gauge or higher numbered wire, which is thinner than the 20 gauge wire, use a different method for beginning or ending the bead unit. Measure about 1 inch from the end of the wire and bend the wire back at a right angle with the flat-nose pliers. This time, place the round-nose pliers at the bend in the wire, not at the end. Repeat the process of twisting the wire half way around and then repositioning the pliers and bending all the way around. The long end of wire that is left is now twisted around the piece of wire that the beads will eventually go on. Hold the circle with a pair of flat nose pliers and hold the piece of wire to be twisted with another pair of flat nose pliers and twist away. Cut off the excess wire. There should be at least three twists done before cutting away the excess. You will get used to holding two pliers and doing an action that requires movement.

When working with any gauge wire in the process of twisting or bending the wire, each end of the wire must be held by pliers. Otherwise, the wire will go in an uneven direction or loose its shape. Wire is very forgiving if it is handled correctly, and unforgiving if it is mistreated. Life is the same way.

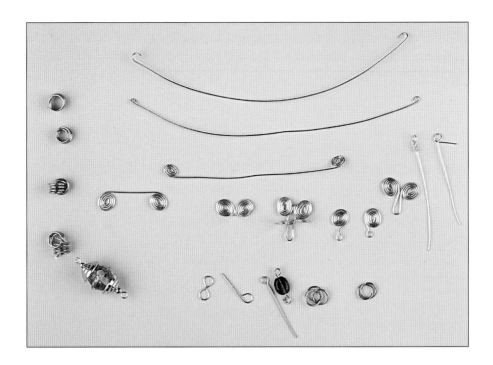

Egyptian Swirls

Egyptian Swirls are an interesting wire design. I have used these swirls for entire necklaces, and in this book I show the use of the swirl in combination with beads.

Cut a 6 ½ inch length of wire. Curve both ends half way around, and then pinch the ends closed. Hold the pinched end with flat-nose pliers and turn the piece of wire to sit along side one edge of the curve. Continue to reposition the pliers and curve along the edge. After a few turns with the pliers you can turn the edge of the wire with your fingers. Consistently alternate coiling one side and then the other side so that both sides are even. Coil each end until the inside length of the wire is 1 ½ inches in length.

With the round nose pliers hold the center point of the inside wire and bend the coils back toward the center. With the flat nose pliers positioned right above the two circles bend the wire down to form a right angle. Using your fingers pinch the wire down flat to the coils. Do this with the beginning unit. For connecting units leave the wire at the right angle and do not fold it flat to the coils. To connect units Insert the piece that is at a right angle into a folded piece and pinch until it is flat. Continue assembling the units to the desired length. In the last unit place a ring instead of another unit. (Helen Clegg and Mary Larom, *Making Wire Jewelry*, "An Ancient Design, Egyptian Swirls", pp 12-18.)

First Rings

The bead units in the book are begun with a ring. When using 20 gauge or lower numbered wire, the following method is used to create the first rings. Measure 3/8 inch from the end of the wire and bend the end back at a right angle. Using round nose pliers that are placed at the end of the wire, twist the wire half way. Reposition the pliers and twist again until the ring is closed. Alternate each side of the wire with one side up and one side down. This is the same method already mentioned for the first circle of the jig. It is something that you will do for almost every piece of jewelry in this book so I felt it was good to give the explanation again.

Chain Patterns

Chain patterns can be single-, double-, or triple-ring units. The single ring unit is the one used the most often. When making the two-ring unit, one ring is placed inside the other ring and the rings are closed together. Make sure that the direction of the rings and the overlapping of the rings is the same for each unit. Three rings connected together create a very pretty chain. Connect the first two rings and then place the third ring inside the first two rings. Again make sure that the all the rings for each unit are going in the same direction. (Irene Peterson, *Great Wire Jewelry*, "Single and Double Flower Chain," pp 34-35.)

After winding the rings around a mandrel and removing the rings from the mandrel you usually cut off one ring at a time. For this chain pattern, bend away a unit of four rounds and cut it free. Make sure that the cut is where the fourth round would complete a full circle. Notice that the first twisted wire begins in the middle of the circle. Cut the last ring off in the middle of the circle. Pinch the ends into the center of the circle with flat nose pliers. Make sure the pliers are smooth on the inside so that the wire doesn't scratch. Twist one ring into the other by folding a single piece of wire around the closed ring until all of the rounds of wire are inside the closed ring. When the ring is attached, pinch the ends into the center. (Helen Clegg and Mary Larom, *Making Wire Jewelry*, "A Simple Chain," pp. 22-24, 34.)

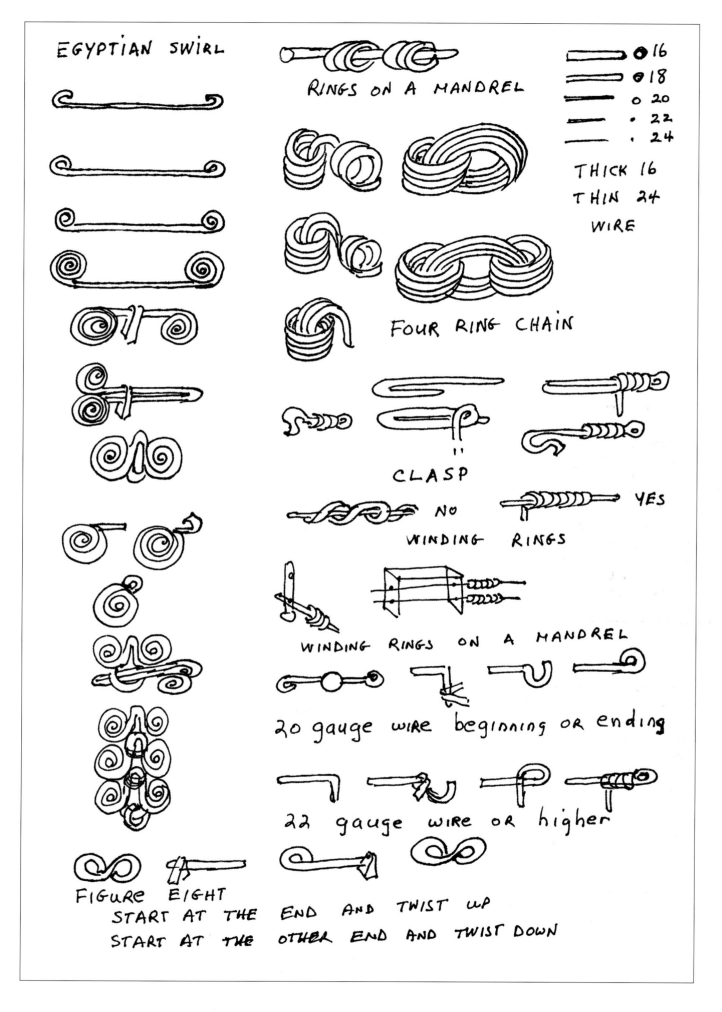

EGYPTIAN SWIRL

RINGS ON A MANDREL

16
18
20
22
24

THICK 16
THIN 24
WIRE

FOUR RING CHAIN

CLASP

NO   YES
WINDING   RINGS

WINDING RINGS ON A MANDREL

20 gauge wire beginning or ending

22 gauge wire or higher

FIGURE EIGHT
START AT THE END AND TWIST UP
START AT THE OTHER END AND TWIST DOWN

4. A Great Place to Begin

Onyx and Tiger Eye

Beautiful black onyx and brown tiger eye beads were attractive all by themselves. All they needed was an interesting chain with enough spacing so that the beads really were the stars.

Materials:
20 gauge sterling silver wire
18 tiger eye beads
32 small silver beads
  2 square silver beads
  2 earring findings

A tiger eye bead surrounded by 2 silver beads and connected by a single ring on each side is the center. The rest of the beads are strung with 2 rings separating each bead, which is surrounded by 2 silver beads. This necklace is simple but eloquent.

The earring has a unit like the necklace, connected by a single ring to a bead that is topped by the square silver bead.

Materials:
20 gauge sterling silver wire
15 black onyx beads
  2 long silver tubes
  6 small silver balls

Surrounding the center bead is a repetition of 4 single and 3 double ring units connected to the bead on either side. 3 single and 2 double ring units, 4 single and 3 double ring units, 3 single and 2 double ring units repeated 3 times. The end unit is 4 single and 3 double ring units.

The earrings have a single unit of a small silver bead, black onyx bead, small silver bead, long silver tube and small silver bead connected to the finding by a 2 double ring unit surrounded by 2 single rings.

Flat Chain Mail

This is one of my favorite chain designs. To begin your experimentation with chain mail, I recommend that you use 2 different colors of wire, which makes it easier to keep track of the rings. Once you conquer making the chains, you will ask yourself, "Why did I think this was going to be difficult to do?" I first heard about this type of chaining from my college student who was into heavy metal music, nose rings, and chain mail worn as gloves

The most important part is to always connect the rings in the same direction, the same ring is over and the same ring is under. Always end both sides with 2 rings, and then one ring, so that a clasp can be attached.

Lay out on the table 3 sets of 2 rings each. Join these sets with 2 rings. Continue this pattern with sets of 3 rings and the 2 rings. I have made full chain mail necklaces, but prefer the chain interspersed with beads. (Irene **Peterson,** *Great Wire Jewelry,* "Flat Chain Mail," p 36.)

Materials
20 gauge silver wire
 6 small onyx round beads
 4 triangle black beads
 2 rectangular swirl beads
 5 small triangle beads with design
 9 head pins
 Assorted small beads to fill the head pin beads to equal lengths
24 small silver beads

Chain mail 7 lines, each with 3 outside rings on each side. Necklace: 13 chain mail units connected by 5 rings with 9 dangles from the center chain mails. .Connect the units as shown, with 7 beaded units on one side, connected with 2 chain mail units. Small bead, triangular bead, chain mail, triangular bead, round bead, rectangular swirl, and 2 bead units.

Double Chain and Egyptian Swirl

This necklace was inspired by wanting a variation on the Egyptian swirls that are continuously linked together, as described in the introduction. Sometimes wire can stand on its own with just a little help from the beads. The lack of color makes this a very easy necklace to wear with anything. Every girl needs a gold chain. This is my affordable, funky gold chain necklace.

Materials:
 2 earring findings
20 gauge gold-filled wire
18 filigree gold beads
 9 gold beads
74 Egyptian swirls, done as a single teardrop

Start by making 8 units as follows: 11 double rings with 2 drops on 5 rings, using every other ring, and with 2 drops on 5 rings using every other ring, and attaching the drops with 2 rings each. Connect with 8 bead units.

The earrings have 6 swirls hanging on the bottom ring.

Chain Units and
Bead Rings Intertwined

This necklace is very light to wear and rather dainty, especially good for wearing in the summer to dress up a simple t-shirt. There is a combination of wires in this necklace that adds a little drama.

Materials:
20 gauge gold-filled wire for part of the chain
20 gauge gold wire for the bead rings
50 small metal beads in green, purple and black or your choice of colors
82 units of 3 rings
29 rings with 2 beads each

After wrapping the wire around the mandrel to create the rings you, usually would cut off one ring at a time, but this time you cut off three rings together. Count 4 lines and then cut.

Twist one unit into the next unit by slightly opening the first ring and placing it inside the next unit and keep on turning until all the unit is inside and connected. Press in and down on the beginning of the ring so it lies flat against the unit. Make these rings not too big, so wrap the wire around a skinny mandrel.

All of the interlocked 3 ring units are connected by a single ring that is a larger size than the rings just made.

Start with 12 units of 3 rings each, then 5 units of 3 done twice, 7 units of 3, and finally 4 units of 3. Reverse the order with 7 units of 3, 5 units of 3 done twice, and 12 units of 3 rings each.

Between each of these units are single rings with 2 beads on each ring. Connect the rings between the beads. First is a 2 unit group followed by a 3 unit, 2 unit, five 3 units, and 2 unit, for a total of 29 units.

The Journey of Turquoise Beads

The turquoise beads were used in many different designs. Each necklace I wore a few times and then realize that I didn't like the design at all. The beads looked too heavy or the beads just didn't show how beautiful they really are but I loved the beads so I kept on designing and finally got it right. This design I loved wearing.

A hint to the person just starting out on the journey of jewelry making is that even artists who have designed jewelry for a long time can run into difficulties.

Materials:
20 gauge gold-filled wire
8 large turquoise beads
9 small iridescent beads
36 small gold beads
2 earring findings
2 6 inches of wire
8 S shaped connectors
6 #5 jig pieces
2 Egyptian Swirls

Follow the pattern for the length of the necklace, but use 3 iridescent beads for the center. Connect with jig pieces 4 times in the center, and then connect 4 times on each side, with S-shaped connectors ending with 2 jig connectors. Use rings before and after every jig piece or an S-shaped piece.

The earring picture shows what the units are and how they are connected. Refer to Egyptian Swirl directions and make only one side, then end with a circle made with the round-nose pliers.

Square Wire Connector

Wire also comes in a square form. Most of the jewelry in this book uses round wire, but square wire off-sets the beads, although its purpose is to connect.

Materials:

20	gauge gold filled round wire
20	gauge gold filled flat wire
9	gold beds with a raised surface
6	faceted bronze beads
2	purple metal beads
30	small green and purple metal beads
14	square wire rings

When working with square wire, be careful that you do not scratch the wire but make clean, sharp cuts when you cut the rings. The pattern of beads is centered, with a gold bead followed by a purple bead, gold bead, bronze bead, 3 gold beads, and 2 bronze beads. Repeat the pattern for the other side starting with a purple metal bead and work backward.

Green Bead
Necklace and Earring

Colors can be monochromatic, as in this necklace with all the beads being green but of different value. The stones also vary in size and shape. All the stones are smooth and translucent in the example.

Materials:

- 10 dark green flat beads
- 7 light green curved bead
- 11 small green oval beads
- 5 Jig # 8
- 6 Jig # 33
- 1 Head Pin
- 4 Gold
- 20 gauge gold-filled wire
- 2 earring findings
- 1 hand made clasp
- 39 small rings

The necklace and its center are shown in the photograph. Connect the units on one side, and repeat backward for the other side.

The Beauty of Square Wire

I don't use square wire often, but when I do the wire is as important as the beads. Rings made with square wire are part pf the design. In one necklace I used both small and large square wire rings. In another necklace I used only large square rings.

The center unit is a large gold bead. Connecting units on each side are small, medium, and small gold beads. All units are connected by a large square wire ring. The next unit on each side is a large gold bead followed by small, medium, and small gold beads repeated 5 times on each side and ending with 6 round gold rings on each side. Even the clasp is made from square wire.

Materials:

20 gauge gold filled round wire
24 gauge gold-filled wires (Note: If the cost of gold wire is an issue, you can always substitute 24 gauge silver wire, as long as the beads aren't too large.)
24 small gold beads
10 medium gold beads
 3 large gold beads

The second necklace has beautiful square beads which work well against the square wire rings.

Materials:

11 square grey /white marble beads
6 round clear beads
34 small reddish purple beads

Alternate 2 purple square grey bead units with a purple clear round bead purple unit. Connect with alternating small and large round wire rings. There are a total of 17 units with a purple square purple unit in the center that is connected with a large square wire ring on each side.

Cloisonné Bead

The cloisonné beads that I bought reminded me of the cloisonné lamp, which I thought was so beautiful that my mother and father had bought in an antique store. I had a hard time coming up with a design that would show case the cloisonné beads. Again these cloisonné beads were used in a few unsuccessful designs before the design that I drew on this page.

Materials:

20 gauge gold filled wire
20 gauge gold filled square wire
12 cloisonné beads
13 Jig # 5 units
42 seed beads a color that compliments the cloisonné
18 oval gold beads
2 large round beads that compliment the cloisonné
26 rings to connect
18 head pins
18 small pearls
18 rectangular beads that compliment the cloisonné

Every unit is identical and is connected with the jig unit and square wire rings. Hanging from one of the curves in the jig unit are 2 head pins with a seed bead, pearl, rectangular bead, and a seed bead. There are 7 units of 2 head pins. The last 2 jig pieces on either side have no head pins.

Wire Chains

Sometimes beads aren't what you want to wear or you can't find any beads that will match an outfit. Chains come to the rescue. These two types of chains I particularly like and wear them often.

Silver Chain

Materials:
20 gauge sterling silver wire
18 gauge sterling silver wire

Continuous units of 4 rounds of wire and ended with 2 rounds of wire and having a total of 79 units of wire, 18 gauge rounds in the center followed by 20 gauge in the back. (Helen Clegg and Mary Larom, *Making Wire Jewelry*, "A Simple Chain," pp. 22-24, 34.)

Silver Chain

Materials:
20 gauge non tarnishing silver wire
2   round silver engraved beads
4   round silver raised beads.

A continuous connection by a single ring, units of 3 rings each that are connected.

Necessity is the mother of invention somebody once said and it is true. This chain necklace was too tight around my neck so I made more of the chain and decided to add the silver beads on either end of my new length of chain and placed this piece in the front of the necklace.

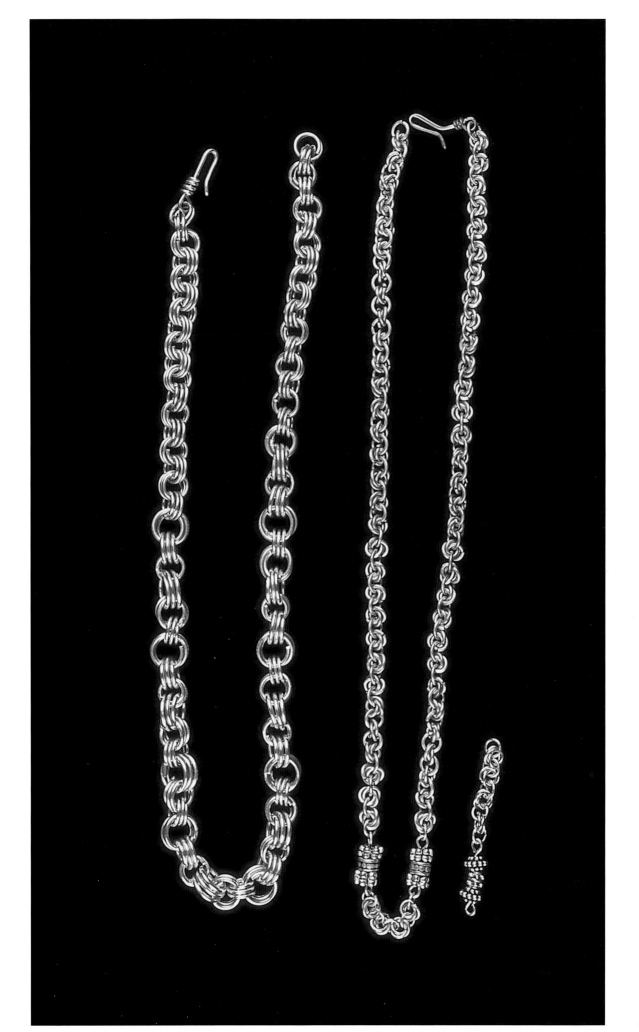

Brown Beads

The brown beads came from my mother's long necklace which she wore wound around her neck twice. This is my version of the brown bead necklace. As I noted in the introduction copper wire is great for experimentation and can also be used for a finished piece of jewelry. In this piece I felt that the copper wire was a perfect complement to the color of the beads.

Materials:
13 Brown beads   A
12 Gold wood beads   B
18 Small brown beads   C
6 Gold Barrels   D
6 Brass beads   E
Jigs number 35 and 16 (Dawn Cusick, *Making Bead and Wire Jewelry*, pp. 90-92.)

Repeat, following the drawing, for the second side of the necklace.

Silver Heart

This silver heart was given to me many years ago when my daughter was in high school by a parent that I met at the school events for parents. The heart was on a piece of rope or cord. I loved the heart but the cord got old looking so the heart stayed in the jewelry box. When I first started making jewelry I forgot about the heart but when I started to write the book I knew that the heart had to be a part of my book. Therefore I designed this piece of jewelry which is all silver just like the heart.

Materials:
20 gauge silver wire
Multiple silver rings
6 small lined silver balls-A
16 medium sized smooth round silver balls -B
6 square silver beads- C
6 medium size lined silver balls-D
4 oblong raised silver beads-E
6 small lined beads-F
4 large round silver balls-G
6 large round lined silver ball-H
4 silver tubes-I
6 findings in silver with 3 holes to string 3 units at once.
1 Heart or something of your choice for the center.-K

"Ring away" was all I could think as I kept on making more rings. The heart has on each side an outside set of 7 rings including the ring that goes through the finding and 2 other sets of 6 rings, which include the ring that goes through the finding. All three rings get another ring each and the last ring joins all three pieces into a single unit.

The first unit on each side is a square bead, a medium sized smooth round silver ball, a large round lined silver ball, a small silver ball, and a square bead. The next unit is a small lined silver bead, large round silver ball, small lined silver bead.

Ring away with three rings in the single unit that was just attached. Each outside unit has 8 rings including the ring in the 3 circle finding. The center unit has two rings attached to a silver tube unit with a single ring at top through the 3 circle finding. Again all three rings get another ring each and the last ring joins all three pieces into a single unit.

The next unit has a medium size lined silver ball, a medium size smooth silver ball, a large lined silver ball, a medium size smooth silver ball, an oblong raised silver bead and a small lined silver ball.

This unit is followed by another single unit. The single unit consists of a small lined silver ball, a medium sized smooth silver ball, a large round silver ball, an oblong raised silver bead and a medium sized smooth silver bead.

Create 3 lines to work from with an attachment of 3 rings. The outside lines have 7 rings including the ring through the 3 ring finding and the inside line has two rings attached to a silver tube unit with a single ring at the top through the 3 circle finding. Add 2 rings to each of the 3 rings and connect with a single ring.

The last unit has a medium size smooth silver ball, large lined silver ball, medium sized lined silver ball, medium size smooth silver ball and a square silver ball. Attach two rings to the last unit and attach with a single ring to the clasp.

When you are done I think that you will feel that all those rings were worth the effort and that going around in circles is some times beneficial.

5. Memories

I remember my mother wearing her pearls with this clasp, which is now the center piece of my necklace. There were two challenges. The first challenge was to find beads that weren't precious which would compliment the clasp which is diamonds, real pearls and sapphires.

The second challenge was to balance the clasp so that I could use the clasp at the front of the necklace. Again, it took a few attempts before I was pleased with the results.

Materials:
20 gauge non-tarnishing wire
10 translucent beads
34 small pearl beads
26 small onyx beads
6 medium onyx beads
10 small silver beads
2 headpins
7 silver beads
4 pink pearl beads

Initial Center

Again, a piece of my mother's jewelry inspired this design, which is an eight-sided polygon in gold with her initials engraved as the center of the necklace. I have tried many ways of surrounding the center and have worn the necklace a few times but was never quite satisfied with the results. I was looking for a funky look to wear with casual clothes, the kind that I wear to teach. I am finally satisfied with this necklace. Don't be afraid to tear apart and redesign it.

Materials:
20 gauge gold-filled wire
1 engraved center (substitute whatever you want)
8 small gold balls
4 raised gold balls
4 lined gold balls
6 gold flowers
4 gold arrows
8 gold lined tubes
8 small gold balls
1 magnetic clasp

Alternate the connections with single rings and double rings.
Unit A is a medium gold ball, a raised gold ball, followed by medium gold ball.
Unit B is a flower
Unit C is an arrow
Unit D is a small gold ball, lined gold tube, lined gold ball followed by a lined gold tube and a small gold ball.

Repeat units B and C followed by Unit A, Unit B, and Unit D.

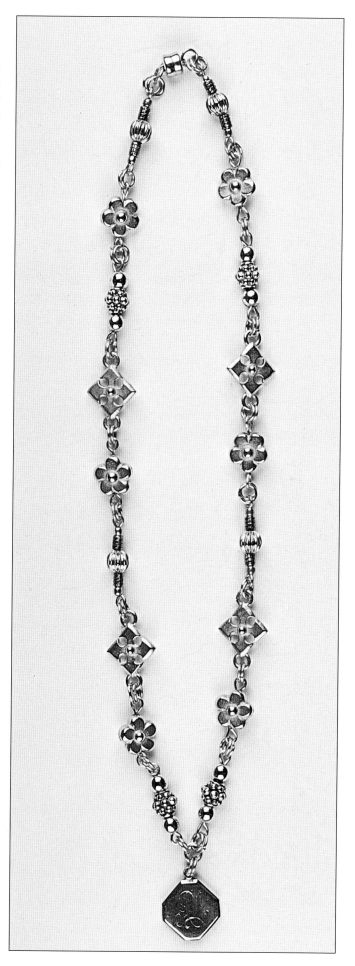

This particular piece is closed by a magnetic clasp that is great for anybody who has a hard time maneuvering the closing of clasps. The clasps that I showed you how to make yourself are also easy to close, which is probably why I use them almost exclusively in my jewelry. It is nice to have beautiful jewelry but a problem if it takes forever to put the jewelry on, especially if you are getting ready for work and are on a tight time schedule, which is usually the case.

Quebec

Whenever we travel, I like to bring back beads from the trip. Quebec, being an artistic a town, had a wonderful small but well stocked bead store near our hotel. The beads that I bought are red, a match with many of my clothes.

Materials:
20 gauge gold filled wire
13 red beads
12 square gold beads
18 small gold beads engraved beads
30 small gold balls
20 small dark red balls
2 t pins
2 earring findings
1 clasp

Assemble 10 units of a small dark red ball on each side of the square gold bead. For the earrings the square gold bead is surrounded by 2 small gold balls.

Assemble 9 units of the engraved gold bead, small gold ball, red bead, small gold bead, engraved gold ball. For the earrings use two gold balls, a red ball and 2 gold balls.

Starting with a center red ball unit and alternate a red ball unit with the square gold bead unit ending with a red ball unit, for the completion of the necklace. The earrings have a square gold bead on the T pin and the red ball on the top. All of the units are assembled with medium size gold rings.

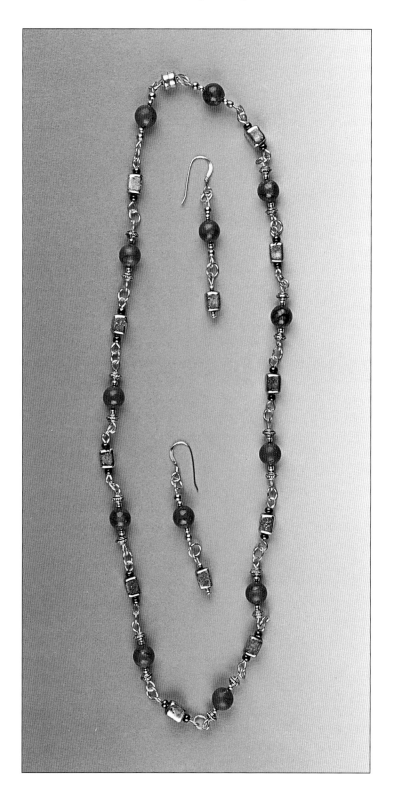

Oregon's Coastline

Whenever we travel we always go antiquing or visit a gallery, museum or any place that has art and particularly art from the region that we are visiting and by a local artist. This store on the gorgeous coastline of Oregon had blown glass beads made by the owner's daughter. I don't do blown glass, so when I saw this bead I had to buy it. The colors and the shape are what I was attracted to. I knew that I would incorporate the bead into my jewelry making. Eventually I did. I remade the necklace many times because I couldn't get the balance of the bead to lay right and the hole in the bead was crocked, but my perseverance was worthwhile. When I do wear this necklace someone always comments in a very positive way.

Repeat the drawing or picture for the other side of the necklace.

Materials:
Pendant Bead
5 Gold flower beads
20 small pearls
 1   small turquoise bead
 1   turquoise heart

6 medium pink beads
4 Gold cross bead
2 large turquoise beads
1   head pin

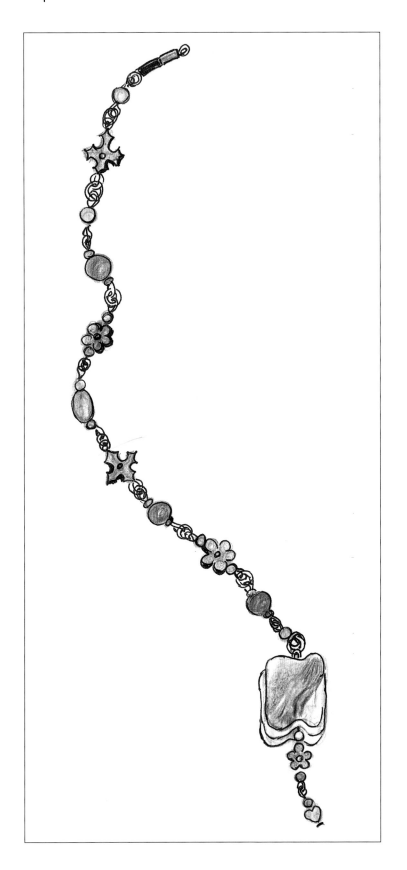

6. Green

A Little Green

Never did I realize how many pieces of jewelry I have made that include green. Welcome to my world of green. beads

Materials:
20 gauge silver wire
28 small silver beads
16 round speckled green oval beads
1 center piece of a green beveled stone
1 magnetic clasp
20 round light green beads
6 oval darker green small beads

Unit A – silver, green speckled bead, round green bead, green speckled bead, silver bead unit.
Unit B- silver, round green, darker green bead, round green bead and silver bead unit.
Alternate Unit A and B for a total of 14 units to complete the necklace

Grey and Green

Materials:
20 gauge sterling silver wire
12 round green beads
8 small bluish green beads
28 small silver beads
12 silver bead caps
4 speckled green beads
2 rectangular green beads
4 brass beads
4 silver multiple ball beads
1 green heart pendant

The units are very varied but repeat on each side. The heart is the center unit which is strung on a series of 3 rings.

The third ring holds the connectors for each side.

Unit A-silver, bluish, green bead, green bead, bluish green bead and silver bead.
Unit B-silver, bead cap, green bead, bead cap, silver
Unit C- brass, speckled green, rectangular green, speckled green, brass
Unit D- Silver, silver multiple ball beads, rectangular green bead, multiple ball bead, silver.
Repeat Unit B, followed by Unit A, Unit B, and Unit A.

Egyptian Style
Dark Green Necklace

I like the balance of silver and green in this necklace and the long green tube beads look like marble, which compliments the engraved tube silver beads.

Materials:

20	gauge sterling silver wire
4	long tube marble looking dark green and black bead
6	oval green beads
2	round green beads
10	medium size green metal beads
20	small green beads
2	square silver beads
22	engraved tube silver beads
6	raised ball silver beads
2	silver flower earring findings

Unit A- Silver square bead, small green bead, oval green bead, small green bead and a silver tube bead

Unit B- medium size green metal bead, silver tube, round green bead, silver tube and medium size green bead

Unit C- small green bead, silver tube, long green and black marble tube, silver tube and small green bead

Unit D- small green bead, raised ball silver bead, oval green bead, raised ball silver bead, and small green bead.

Unit E- small green bead, medium size green metal bead, silver tube, oval green bead, silver tube, medium size green bead and small green bead.

Unit F- small green bead, medium metal green bead, raised ball silver bead, and small green bead

Unit G- medium metal green bead, silver tube, oval green bead, silver tube and small green bead.

All connections are a single medium sized ring.

For the necklace connect the 2 unit A's together with the square silver beads facing each other. Now connect unit B, Unit C, Unit D, Unit B and Unit E. for each side.

For the earrings string on a T-pin, Unit F, and connect to Unit G which is connected to the finding.

43

Onward with Green

These green beads I really love. The shape and the internal design are intriguing and eye catching. There is nothing dull about these beads.

Materials:
20 gauge sterling silver wire
13 rectangular green beads
34 brass beads
4   small dark green beads
34 small green and purple metal beads

Because the beads themselves are so beautiful the design of the necklace is almost a constant repeat except for the last 2 units which are Unit B.
Unit A is green purple metal bead, brass bead, rectangular green bead, brass bead and green purple metal bead. Make 13 units.
Unit B is the same as A except that the center bead is a small round dark green bead.
The earrings are a combination of Unit A first and then Unit B strung on a head pin.
The connectors throughout are medium silver rings.

More Green

Materials:
20 gauge sterling silver wire
Jig #'s 24 and 25
Jig # 6 for center
Egyptian Swirls
32 small oval green beads
16 silver ball beads
2 large oval green beads
2 irregular shaped green bead
2 light green beads
2 small purple beads
2 small gold balls

The center is Jig # 24 or 25 hanging from Jig #6 with the enclosed green bead which is attached to Jig # 24 or 25 Unit A is a small oval green bead, silver ball bead and small oval green bead which is the first unit used.
Unit B is an oval green bead.
Unit C is Jig #24 or 25
Unit D is Egyptian Swirl .This is a single unit of the Egyptian Swirl that is unattached.

Start with Unit A, B, and C. Then use 3 Unit A's followed Unit D and then 4 Unit A's.

The earrings are one unit strung on a T pin with purple, irregular green, small oval green, light green, small oval green and small gold ball which is attached to an earring finding.

45

The Last of Green

Materials:

20 gauge gold-filled wire,
one medium green bead,
4 irregular shaped green and black bead
22 small light green beads
4 gold bead fillers
18 small gold beads
2 small purple beads
8 small black beads
8 medium green beads
2 green flower beads
4 large black beads
2 speckled green beads
8 dark green beads
6 small round green beads
4 small white beads

This is a combination of leftovers that I think works well. The connectors are a 3-ring chain surrounded by 2 medium gold rings. The length of the connectors allows the various combinations to have space to be seen and balanced in appearance against the connectors.

The center is a gold bead, a small speckled green bead, a medium green bead, a small green bead and a gold bead. Unit A is next with small purple, small light green, irregular shaped green, light green and small purple. Unit B is dark green, light green, dark green, gold bead. Unit C is gold, light green, gold filler, small round green, gold filler, light green, gold.
Repeat Unit A, and repeat Unit B
Unit D- the last unit is small black metal bead, light green, large black metal bead, small black metal bead.

Earrings

The earrings are two units. On the T-pin are a small white bead, small black metal bead, large black metal bead, small black metal bead, light green bead small green bead, small round green bead, small white bead. Attached by a ring are a small black bead, green flower bead, and a small black bead.

7. Purple

Purple Antique

Tthis jewelry has an inherited center piece that belonged to my mother and was given to her by her aunt Cecelia. The piece was a part of a choker necklace that I knew I'd never wear. I took the necklace apart and played. The following are my results.

Materials:
10 translucent purple, heart beads
20 gauge gold wire
44 small purple beads
10 medium size round beads
20 gold bead sides
  4 oval purple beads
  4 medium size metal purple beads
  2 faceted round medium size purple beads
  2 faceted round small size purple beads
48 small purple beads

When you are shopping, the important thing to remember is the difference in sizes of the beads and the variation in the material of the bead that gives a variety in value of the color. This attention to detail adds to the design of the jewelry. If you don't like purple or have a piece for the center that is a different color, just adapt the directions for materials to buy.

The two outermost sides hanging off the pendant were added on. On a T-pin put small purple bead, oval purple bead, medium size metal purple bead, and a small purple bead.

Unit A- small purple, heart, small purple. Make 10.
Unit B- small purple, gold bead, medium round bead, gold bead, small purple. Make 10.

Alternate Unit A and Unit B starting with Unit A. One side of the necklace should have 10 units. All then units are connected with a single round medium size ring.

Pearls and Purple Barrel Beads

Materials:
20 gauge gold wire
20 gauge copper wire
1 large round Metal, Purple Bead
6 medium sized, round, metal, purple beads
12 small pearls
22 small brass beads
30 very small brass beads
30 very small black beads

Unit A- very small black bead, very small brass bead, small brass bead on either side of a large, round, metal, purple bead

Unit B- very small black bead, very small brass bead, small brass bead on either side of a pearl, brass, pearl bead

Unit C- very small black bead, very small brass bead, medium size round, metal, purple bead

Unit D- very small black bead, very small brass bead, small brass bead, on either side of a small pearl

All the units are strung on 20 gauge copper wire and are connected with a medium size gold ring. The center is unit A. On each side, attach Unit B, Unit C, Unit D, Unit C, Unit B, Unit C, and Unit B.

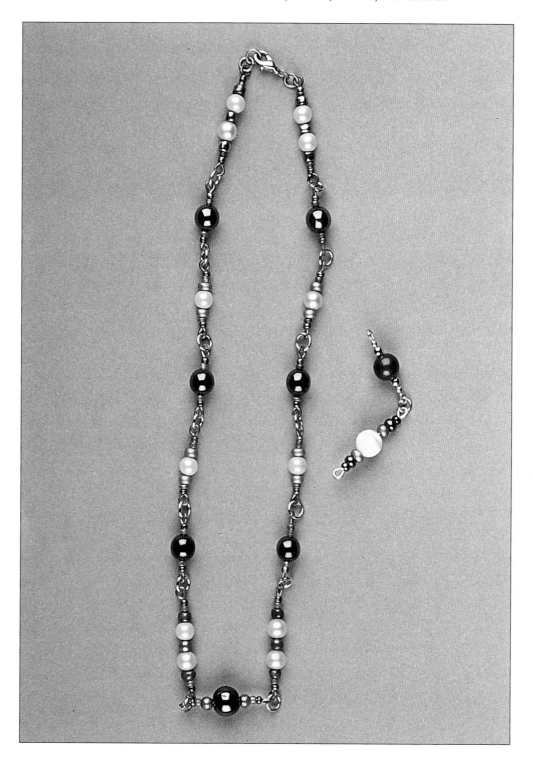

More Purple Barrel Beads

Materials:

20	gauge gold-filled wire
10	medium size purple metal barrel beads
2	raised circle gold beads
1	gold lined circle bead
1	gold lined oblong bead
3	raised oblong purple beads
24	small metal beads
14	seed bead size metal beads
2	earring findings
2	T-pins
16	very small gold beads
4	medium size gold beads

This is a variation of the first design using some of the same beads. I am always delighted to see how different the beads look when placed in a different setting. Color does the same thing when placed next to other colors.

Unit A- raised oblong purple bead surrounded by 2 very small gold beads. Make 3.

Unit B- Small metal bead, Barrel bead, small, metal bead. Make 10.

Unit C- small, gold bead, small metal bead, small, gold bead, small metal bead, and small gold bead. Make 6.

Unit D- seed size metal bead, small metal bead gold lined circle bead or oblong lined gold bead, small metal bead, and seed bead size metal bead. Make 2, one with the circle and one with the oblong gold bead.

Unit E- small gold bead, small metal bead, medium size gold bead, raised circle gold bead- strung on a T-pin for the bottom of the earring drop.

Start in the center with Unit A and surround the unit on each side with Unit B followed by Unit A. On each side attach Unit D, Unit C, Unit A, Unit C, Unit A, Unit C and end with Unit A. All of the units are attached with a medium gold ring.

For the earrings attach a Unit A to the earring finding with medium gold ring and Unit E which is on the T-pin to unit A with another medium gold ring.

Purple Metal and Translucent Beads with Pearls

How to make a necklace with a few left over beads added to a new bead is what this necklace is about. It forces the designer to be innovative but is also helpful because there is a limit to the quantity of each kind of bead. Whenever there is a limit of anything people must be more innovative in coming up with a solution.

Materials:
20 gauge gold wire
20 gauge copper wire
1   large metal purple round bead
2   metal barrel beads
14   small pearls
41   very small black and purple beads
4   square, translucent, purple beads

Unit A- alternate the use of the very small black and purple bead. A small black or purple bead, large round metal purple bead and a small black or purple bead

Unit B- A pearl surrounded by either a small purple or black bead

Unit C- Metal Barrel surrounded by either a small black or purple bead.

Unit D- Translucent, Square, Purple bead surrounded by either a small black or purple bead.

All the units are strung on 20 gauge gold wire and connected by medium size copper rings.

The center is Unit A. On either side of unit A are Unit B followed by Unit C. Unit D. Unit C, Unit D, and 4 Unit Cs

Purple and White

The beads that are oblong are beautiful purple to white fade, and the smaller beads are translucent purple and white. The oval purple bead with a small black line also does a fade of one color to another. These beads were bought at a bead show, which is always a wonderful experience but quite overwhelming. To be surrounded by tables and tables of beads makes you dizzy. I usually do a walk through sometimes a few times before I actually look at individual beads and start to fill my tray. I always buy a lot and spend more than I planned on spending and my adoring husbands response when I complain about how much I spent is did you enjoy yourself? Of course I did and my stash gives me months of enjoyment as I create my jewelry.

Materials:
6 oblong purple and white bead
6 oval purple beads with a black line
8 engraved silver beads
8 thin oval circle silver beads
4 translucent purple beads
1 gold circle bead
12 small silver beads
2 small dark purple beads
20 gauge sterling silver wire

Because of the beauty of the beads I wanted to have space between and the wire to act as beads. What I did was create flower chains which is 3 rings connected and is explained with the different chains and then connected these flower chains with a single ring.

The center is a small silver bead, purple bead with the black line, gold circle bead, purple bead with the black line and a small silver bead. Connected on either side are single chain, flower chain, single chain, flower chain and a single chain.

Unit A- silver bead, oblong purple/white bead, silver bead. Make 6.
Unit B- engraved silver bead, thin silver bead, oval purple bead with the black line, thin silver bead, engraved silver bead. Make 4.
Unit C- translucent purple bead. Make 4.

Alternate Unit A with Unit B and Unit A with Unit C, and end with Unit A. All the chains, except the last one that connects to the clasp, are two flower rings connected by 3 single rings. At the end, use one flower chain connected by 2 single rings before attaching the clasp.

The earrings are a Unit B on a T-pin, connected by a single silver ring to a Unit C, connected to the earring finding by a single ring.

Purple Metal Beads

One of my favorite colors is purple. The shiny metal beads came from various sources, including jewelry taken apart.

The center necklace with the multiple hangings is one that I wear a lot. When I made the necklace the style was very popular with teens. The 13 pendants are a variety of small beads that are strung on T pins and attached to the chain with a single ring. The front of the chain is figure 8 shapes attached by single rings. The pendant hangs from the single ring.

A figure 8 is made by using your round nose pliers and with 2 separate turns creating a circle. Place the round nose pliers at the end of the circle along the piece of wire and not the opening. Make another circle as you did the first one but going in the opposite direction.

Materials:
20 gauge gold filled wire.
8   medium barrel metal beads
16 copper flower beads
16 small metal beads
16 seed bead size metal beads.
13 T-pins

The end of the chain that holds the Pendants is a figure eight and then a ring which attaches to the first unit. Unit A – seed bead size metal bead, small metal bead, copper flower bead, medium barrel bead, copper flower bead, small metal bead and seed bead size metal bead. This is the only unit used and 4 are attached to each side of the center and to each other with a single ring. The rings attaching the front are small and the rings attaching the side unit A's are medium.

Purple
Blown Glass Beads

The beads in this necklace remind me of my paper-weight collection, which is all of blown glass.

Materials:
20 gauge sterling silver wire
3 large blown glass beads
2 pink translucent beads
10 pink oval beads
4 small round pink and purple beads
2 oblong pink beads
2 pink tubes
1 purple large oval bead
2 translucent pink tube beads
1 oblong purple translucent bead
6 pink stone rings
8 small purple beads
2 silver square beads
2 earring findings with a silver flower
2 jig pieces

Make a loop and place on the jig, push a bead onto the wire, wrap the wire around the left peg and then around the right peg , push up a bead onto the wire and wrap around a peg that is a distance down but directly under the placement of the first loop.

The center is an oval pink bead, a pink stone ring, large blown glass bead, pink stone ring and oval pink bead. On each side attach a small purple stone, pink translucent bead and purple stone to each side of the center piece. The next unit is a repeat of the center piece for each side, followed by a jig unit and ending with a small purple stone, round pink or purple bead, small purple stone. A total of 9 units are connected for the necklace.

The first 2 chains are 3 small rings, single medium size ring, 3 ring flower, single, medium size ring and 3 small rings. This chain is repeated again for each side. The next chain is 3 small rings, medium single ring, 3 small rings and the last chain is 3 small rings, single medium size ring, 3 ring flower, single medium ring, 3 ring flower, medium single ring and 3 small rings. The last chain is 3 small rings and a medium ring.

Each earring has 2 units. The T-pin units are identical, with oval pink bead, oblong pink bead, and square silver bead. The 2 top units are different, and use ovals, tubes, and whatever beads you haven't used yet. The order doesn't matter. Connect with medium silver rings.

Purple and Hearts

Two of the things that I love are the color purple and the shape of a heart both in symbolism and form. This is a light necklace with translucent light purple shaped beads. The variety of shapes and the use of both gold and silver add contrast with the repetition of unit forms that creates a unity.

Whenever I buy a group of the same beads I save a few for future use with other beads that are found later. This gives me a wonderful stash of a variety of beads that I can make work as a whole and yet have interesting parts.

Materials:
20 gauge non-tarnishing silver wire.
8 translucent purple bells
6 gold balls
6 faceted brass balls
3 translucent purple flowers
4 round translucent purple beads
2 rectangular translucent purple beads
2 large faceted translucent purple beads
2 darker purple hearts
28 small silver beads
2 small gold beads
8 small dark purple beads
Medium size silver rings as connectors.

Create a center unit of gold, silver, flower, silver and gold beads. Connect all units with a medium size silver ring. Create two of each of the following units for each side of the necklace.

Unit A - silver bead, bell, gold bead, round purple bead and silver .
Unit B - silver bead, purple bead, rectangular purple bead, purple bead and silver bead.
Unit C- silver, bell, brass and silver beads.
Unit D - purple, gold, purple flower, gold and purple
Unit E - silver, round purple, gold, round purple and silver.
Unit F- silver, round purple, gold, round purple and silver.
Unit G- same as unit C

The earrings are one unit of silver bead, larger purple bead and silver bead. This is connected to the darker silver heart, which is strung on wire with a wrap closing loop and attached to the unit above with a ring.

59

Recovery Necklace

This was my first attempt at making jewelry after spinal surgery. I would sit at the dining room table and occupy my mind with creating jewelry. This necklace uses inexpensive assorted small purple beads and silver wire.

Materials:
20 gauge silver wire or you could substitute copper wire
Assorted purple beads
A jig either store bought or made by hammering nails with heads to a piece of wood.

Create 12 units with assorted small beads on silver wire. Connect three units with a single small ring on each side. Next attach a jig unit with a single ring on each side.

The next unit is on silver wire and longer than the other units with enough wire left to play on the jig. Attach a jig piece to the last jig piece with 2 rings and hang a t pin of assorted bead. The next jig piece is bigger followed by an attachment with a small ring to the center jig piece which is twisted in a curve of beads and repeated on the other side so that the two units are attached by a small ring on top and on each side a ring attaches the long curved circle of beads that is the pendant hanging in the center. Where the curve of beads meets the previous jig piece again with a T-pin attach an assortment of beads.

I had no game plan. It is one of my funkiest looking pieces and a very free design. Maybe before you start any piece of jewelry in this book you should make a free piece with not so many rules. Learn to create a unit, and how to connect the units and play with the jig and whatever happens just let it have a life.

 8. Pearls

Pearls in Style

Freshwater pearls are beautiful for the irregularity of their shape. They are easy to find in any major chain store that sells craft and art supplies. Although the bead isn't always very small, the hole in the bead is usually tiny and therefore necessitates the use of 24 gauge wire. The pearls in these necklaces are grey, white, and pink.

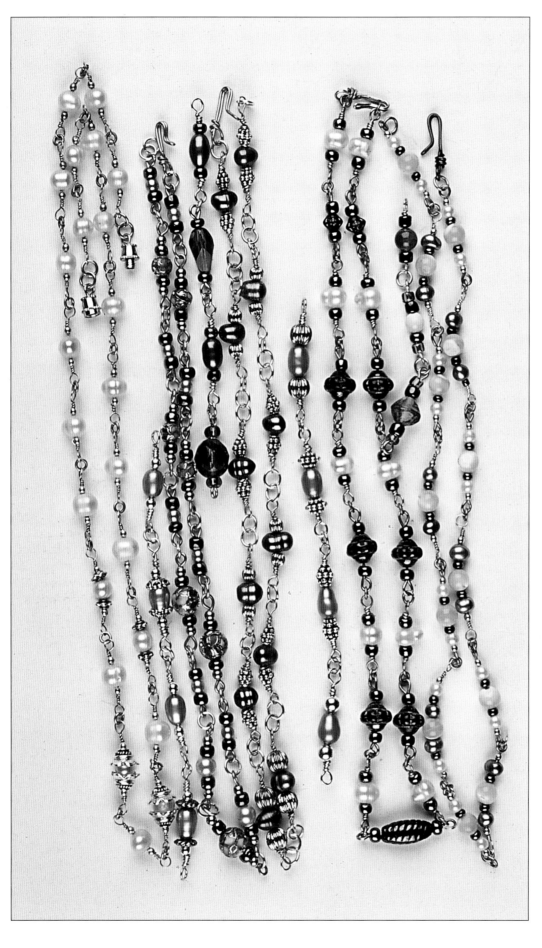

Left

Materials:
23 pink freshwater pearls
4 silver bead caps
24 gauge silver wire
20 gauge silver wire
4 silver round ball beads
46 small silver beads
Barrel Silver Clasp

Long in length, this necklace is easy to make.

Unit A- small silver bead, pearl, small silver bead. Make 19 Unit As.
Unit B- small silver bead, silver bead cap, pearl, silver bead cap, small silver bead. Make 2 Unit Bs.
Unit C- small silver bead, silver round ball bead, pearl, silver round ball bead, small silver bead.

The center is a Unit A with Unit b connected to each side. Follow with a Unit A and then Unit C, followed by 8 Unit A's. Repeat Unit A, then Unit C, Followed by 8 Unit A's for the other side. All the units are connected with a small silver ring.

2nd from the Left

Materials:
20 gauge silver wire
3 large cloisonné beads
4 medium cloisonné beads
2 medium white pearls
8 small pink pearls
34 assorted small metal beads in dark red and green
18 small silver beads
Hand made clasp

The pearls in this necklace aren't fresh water, so I could use 20 gauge wires. All the support beads compliment the cloisonné beads which are white, pink, green and silver. It is a short necklace but packed with brilliance from these colors.

Unit A- silver, metal bead, large cloisonné, metal and silver. Make 3.
Unit B- metal, pink pearl, metal. Make 8.
Unit C – silver, metal, small cloisonné bead, metal, silver. Make 4.
Unit D- silver, metal, medium white pearl, metal silver. Make 2.

All the units are connected with a single, medium-size ring. Starting with a Unit A in the center, attach unit D on either side. Follow with Unit B, Unit A, Unit B, Unit C, Unit B Unit C and ending with Unit B. Repeat these units for the other side.

Center

Materials:
24 gauge sterling silver wire
20 gauge sterling silver wire
12 grey fresh water pearls
4 medium sized round lined silver beads
12 raised ball silver beads
8 small sized round lined silver beads
Hand made clasp

Three Units are used in this necklace, which is short and very light weight.
Unit A- medium lined silver ball, pearl, medium lined silver ball.
Unit B- raised ball silver bead, pearl, raised ball silver bead.
Unit C- small lined silver bead, pearl, small lined silver bead.

The chain is single medium size rings which start with 3 rings, 2 rings and then 1 ring, 2 rings, 3 rings. Connect the 2 Unit As with 3 rings, Unit B with 2 rings and Unit C with 1 ring. The rest of the necklace is Units B, C, B following the order given above for the chain.
Just a reminder: When using the 24 gauge wire, you have to make a loop and then wrap the wire.

Right of Center

Materials:
24 gauge silver wire
20 gauge silver wire
10 white fresh water pearls
6 medium black flower beads
2 small black flower beads
40 small metal black beads
1 oblong lined black bead
Handmade Clasp

Each of the units uses a small black metal bead as the beginning and ending of the unit. The units with then freshwater pearls are strung on the 24 gauge wire and the units with the black beads are strung on the 20 gauge black wire. All the units are connected with small silver rings.

Unit A has the oblong lined black bead.
Unit B has the medium black flower bead.
Unit C has the small black flower bead.
Unit D has the freshwater pearl.

Unit A is in the center. The pattern for each side is Unit D, Unit B, Unit D, Unit B, Unit D, Unit B, Unit D, Unit C, and Unit D.

Far Right

Materials:
24 gauge silver wire
20 gauge copper wire
13 beige and white medium sized beads
26 small silver beads
26 small black and dark red beads
16 small white pearls
12 grey freshwater pearls
Handmade clasp

Unit A- small silver bead, small white pearl, black or dark red bead, beige and white medium sized bead, small white pearl, small silver bead.
String this unit on the copper wire
Unit B- small silver bead, grey pearl, black or dark red bead, beige and white bead, black or dark red bead, grey pearl and small silver bead.
String this unit on the silver wire. Again remember that this is 24 gauge wires so use the loop and twist method for beginning and ending the unit.
Starting with a Unit A in the center, alternate Unit A with Unit B for each side.
All the units are connected with a small copper wire ring.

Pink and Sassy

I was drawn to the unusual color of pink and the see-through quality of these beads. An entire necklace of just these beads would not have worked. They needed a partner to provide contrast. The silver flat beads were just the thing. The pendant allowed me to use 3 beads that were entirely different. Often I buy individual beads and put away a few of each of the beads that I work with for future use. The design of the necklace is the most important part. A poorly designed piece of jewelry doesn't compliment even expensive beads.

Materials:
20 gauge sterling silver wire
8 assorted pink beads. My combination is 4 circles, 2 tubes, 1 translucent circle and 1 translucent flower
10 Egyptian silver beads
1 round engraved silver bead
2 tiny inscribed silver beads
1 tiny silver ball
29 small silver beads
Jig piece of any design that can hold the drop and have the engraved silver ball and small silver ball on top.

The pendant is connected with 2 double rings, 1 single ring and 2 double rings for each side. The Pendant is a silver inscribed ball, pink translucent bead and silver inscribed ball on a T-pin. They are connected with a silver ring to 1 translucent pink flower, that in turn is connected to the jig piece with 3 units of rings described already.

Unit A- silver ball, Egyptian bead, silver ball
Unit B- pink circle bead
Unit C- small silver bead, pink tube, small silver bead

String Unit A, Unit B, Unit A, Unit C, Unit A, Unit B 2 times to finish the body of the necklace. All the units are connected with medium size silver rings.

Old and New but Dressy All the Way

Some of the beads I used are new and some came from my mother-in-law and great aunt. I used the copper wire with the older beads since the color of the bead is very off white. Silver wire was used with the glass beads and rose colored pearl beads. In each piece of jewelry there are interesting interruptions to the beads. The first necklaces are the new.

Far Left

Materials:
24 small pearls with a smooth surface
 8 large pearls with a bumpy surface
20 gauge copper wire

All the beads are strung solo. The units are connected with small copper wire rings.

Second from Left

Materials:
20 gauge silver wire
9 large pink glass beads
10 small pink glass beads
6 silver discs
2 silver tubes
2 gold lined beads
14 white pearls

The large pink glass beads are strung solo. The small pink glass beads are also strung solo. There are 4 units of pearl, silver disc, pearl. Two units are very different with silver tube, pearl, gold bead, pearl, silver disc, pearl.

Center a large pink bead and then attach a pearl, silver disc, pearl, small pink glass, large pink glass, small pink glass, large pink, small pink glass, funky silver tube, pearl, gold bead, pearl, silver disc, pearl, small pink glass bead, large pink, pearl, silver disc, pearl and end with a large pink glass. Repeat this lineup for the other side. Connect with medium size rings.

Center

Materials:
20 gauge sterling silver wire
9 rose colored pearls
2 light rose colored transparent oblong beads
4 small pink glass beads
22 short silver engraved tubes
8 silver discs
8 ribbed silver beads
30 very small silver beads

Unit A- small silver bead, silver tube, rose colored pearl, silver tube, small silver bead. Make 9
Unit B- ribbed silver bead, silver disc, glass pink bead, silver disc, ribbed silver bead. Make 4
Unit C- sm. silver bead, short silver tube, light rose colored transparent bead, short silver tube and sm. silver bead.

Unit A is the center of the necklace. On either side is a Unit B followed by a Unit A and Unit C. Unit B and the last 2 are Unit A. Each side has 7 units. Repeat the order of the units for the other side.

Right of Center

Materials:
26 rose colored pearls
9 gold raised circles bead
6 seed bead size silver beads.

Yes, you have seen these beads before. They really do look different depending on how the beads are strung. Here the only interruptions are the gold beads and a few small silver beads.

Unit A- rose colored pearl strung solo. Make 8
Unit B- seed size silver bead, pearl, gold bead, pearl, seed size silver bead. Make 9.

Alternate Unit B with Unit A, starting with Unit B.

Far Right

Materials:
20 gauge copper wire
20 gauge silver wire
16 small very light pink pearls
14 small off white pearls
4 medium size light pink pearls
1 medium size pink teardrop pearl
12 small clear beads with a pink inside
8 small gold beads

The teardrop is solo and on a medium-size ring, which is used throughout the necklace.

Unit A- The medium size pink pearls are surrounded by gold beads.
Unit B- 2 units of the small off-white pearls.
Unit C- Light pink pearls and the clear beads with pink inside surround the small off white pearls.
Unit D- Clear beads with pink inside surround small white pearls.

String D, A, D, A, B, C, C, C, C. Repeat for the other side.

❧ 9. Black and Silver ❧

Black and Silver, Dressy or Casual

Every woman has in the closet a simple black dress and a black top with black slacks that goes with everything. I like black and feel that I look well in black, so these necklaces have been worn often. The necklaces described are in the picture from the left to the right of the page.

Left

Materials:
20 gauge sterling silver wire
8 small black beads
18 short tube black beads
21 small black metal beads
1 larger metal black bead
2 faceted black beads (shiny)
4 small silver beads
2 flower black beads
4 oval matte black beads
1 silver tube
3 different sized round flat silver beads
4 different jig pieces connected by small silver rings. Jig 13- 15-16-26.
2 shiny silver beads
2 shiny silver wavy tubes
2 raised oblong black beads

The pendant is on a T-pin with the 3 different size round flat silver beads. After the jig units are connected with small silver rings, hang the pendant with a small ring and attach 2 small rings to either side of the top of the jig pieces.

What makes this necklace interesting is that the units are all varied, except for the sameness from side to side.

Unit A- small black, short tube, small metal black, oval black matte, metal black, short tube, small black.
Unit B- small, black, tube black, small silver, flower black, small silver, tube black, small black
Unit C- metal black, tube, small black, shiny silver, faceted black, wavy silver tube, metal black, small black.

Unit D- small black, short tube, metal black, oval matte black, metal black, short tube, small black.
Unit E- small black, short tube, black metal, raised oblong black bead, black metal, short tube and small black.

Connect the Units in the order given from A to E for each side.

Right

Materials:
20 gauge sterling silver wire
2 large shiny black onyx wavy beads
11 Egyptian silver beads
8 small black beads
2 drum shape silver beads
4 small black beads
1 fancy clasp

This is a short necklace and is connected with small silver rings throughout.

Unit A- The large shiny black onyx wavy bead that is strung alone. Make 2.
Unit B- the small black bead which is strung alone. Make 8.
Unit C- the Egyptian silver bead which is also strung alone. Make 11.
Unit D- the silver drum bead that is surrounded by 2 small black beads. Make 2.

I usually don't list clasps in the Materials list, because I make most of my clasps and the directions to make your own clasp are on page 11, but here I bought and used a fancy clasp.

Alternate Unit C and Unit B twice, and end with a Unit C. On each side, attach Unit A. Next attach a Unit B, Unit C, Unit D, Unit C, Unit B twice, ending with a Unit C. The necklace has a total of 23 units.

Black Onyx Beads with Donuts

These black onyx beads are quite unusual, and were mixed with beads that I had. Remember, you can change the beads used, but follow the design.

Left

Materials:

20   gauge sterling silver wire
14   large round black rings (donuts)
16   small purple beads with a center black line
 2   rectangular black beads
 2   black teardrops
 1   large black center bead
 2   braided silver beads
 2   earring findings
 2   engraved silver beads

Repeat the pattern in the drawing once, then use 5 rings to connect a single donut three times, and end with 2 rings.

For the earrings, use the teardrop, small purple beads, and rectangular black beads.

Stars

It is hard to give this necklace a title, since the beads are an unusual color of grayish purple and translucent, but I love the stars in the earrings.

Materials:

20 gauge sterling silver wire
9 grey purple translucent oval beads
26 gold beads
26 small purple beads
14 large purple beads
10 pink beads
2 black onyx hearts
2 black onyx stars
2 burgundy medium size metal beads
2 purple beads with a black line +
4 small silver beads
2 gold tube beads

Unit A – small purple, gold, grey purple, gold, small purple. Make 7.

Unit B- large purple, gold, pink, gold, large purple. Make 6.

Unit C- small purple, gold tube bead, pink, small purple, heart, small purple. Make 2.

String with a Unit A in the center. Connect Unit B on each side. Next add Unit C to each side. Follow with Unit A, Unit B, Unit A, Unit B, Ending with Unit A.

All of the units are connected with a small gold ring.

Earrings

The earrings have 2 drops. The first unit on a t Pin is large purple bead, gray purple bead, small purple beads. The next T-pin unit is a small silver bead, burgundy medium size metal bead, small silver bead. Added to this by a small gold ring is another unit which is strung on the 20 gauge wire of a small purple bead, star, small purple bead, pink bead, small purple bead. The 2 units are connected to the earring finding with 2 large gold rings.

10. Dangles

Funky Silver and Copper Beads

This necklace is different from any of the other pieces of jewelry in this book, because of the consistently large size of the beads and the unique engraved copper beads. Where do you find unique beads? Once you are known to friends, relatives, and acquaintances as a jewelry maker, you will be surprised at the gifts that come your way. A friend of mine worked in a store that was no longer carrying jewelry. Somehow the beads were apart and I got the gift of the unique copper beads.

Materials:
24 gauge silver wire
10 large, lined and raised silver beads
4 flat embossed copper beads
2 large round embossed copper beads
1 medium size dark purple round metal bead
34 small black and dark red metal beads

String each of the beads on 24 gauge wire. Remember that the ends get twisted around. On each side of every bead is a small black or dark red metal bead. I put the lone purple bead in the center and then used a silver bead in between each of the copper beads ending up with 2 silver beads at the end. The units are connected with a small copper ring.

Earrings
For the earrings: 6 medium size copper rings.
On each ring are beads. Lowest ring has 3 silver beads. The ring is connected to the next ring with a small ring that sits between 2 silver beads so that all three silver beads are below the connecting ring. The next ring has 4 metal dark red and black beads and 2 medium size rings connect to the next ring with 2 beads to each side of the rings and a bead in between the 2 rings. The 2 rings connect to the last ring with 4 beads of copper and gold and 2 on each side of the 2 connecting rings. The last ring is also attached to the earring finding.

Long Tiger Eye

Materials:

20 gauge gold wire
56 medium size brown tiger eye beads
36 gold rings
50 sm. Seed beads in black and dark red
14 sm. Gold beads
12 sm. Black and red metal bead
4   lined gold tube
4 flat dark red metallic tubes

Unit A- 3 medium size brown tiger eye beads separated by and beginning and ending with gold rings. Make 4.

Unit B- seed bead, lined gold tube, seed bead, tiger eye, seed bead, lined gold tube, seed bead. Make 2.   Unit C- seed bead, gold disc, tiger eye, gold disc, gold bead, gold disc, tiger eye, gold disc, seed bead. Make 2.

Unit D- seed bead, tiger eye, seed bead, tiger eye, seed bead. Make 2.

Unit E- 4 tiger eye separated by gold beads and sm. metal beads with a flat red tube bead in the center Make 4.

Unit F- gold bead, tiger eye, gold bead, tiger eye, metal bead Make 2.

Center Unit- small gold bead, 3 different discs (copper, gold balls, flat gold) and 2 tiger eyes. Make 1.

Put the Center Unit with Unit D, Unit C, Unit B, Unit C, Unit E, Unit C, Unit F, Unit E.

Repeat the Units in the same order for the other side of the necklace.

Earrings

6 medium size gold rings are connected to the earring finding. Connected to the fourth ring are two different T-pins (#1 and #2) and the last T-pin (#3) is connected to the 6th ring with another ring.

T-pin #1- seed bead, long copper tube, seed bead, metal bead, tiger eye and metal bead.

T-pin #2- seed bead, tiger eye, gold disc, metal bead, seed bead, gold bead, tiger eye, gold disc, seed bead.

T pin #3- seed bead, gold disc, tiger eye, gold disc, gold bead, metal bead, tiger eye, dark red metallic tube, seed bead.

Long and Dangling

I happen to love long, dangling earrings. I don't know why, because I don't have a long swan neck and therefore the earrings almost touch my shoulders. Because I usually wear my hair up or pulled back from my face, the earrings have no competition. The beads in this necklace and earrings come from two necklaces. The large pinkish white bead is from mother, and the small pinkish white bead is from my mother-in-law. None of these beads are precious stones, but I love them for the memories.

Materials:
20 gauge gold wire
13 large pinkish white beads
28 small black onyx beads
34 large rings
24 gauge silver wire
2   medium size pearls
2   earring findings
222 small sized pink and white beads.
2   small size pearls

Unit A- 15 beads alternating small black and small pinkish white beads starting with the small black bead. Make 10
Unit B- 9 beads alternating small black and small pinkish white beads again starting with the small black bead. Make 2
Unit C- 12 beads starting with a small black bead and alternating the small pinkish white bead four times and then a medium size pearl followed by a small black onyx bead.
Unit D- black onyx bead, large pinkish white bead, black onyx bead. String on a T pin.

Start with Unit D in the center, followed by Unit B and then alternating Unit D and Unit A, 9 times, ending with Unit D. Attach with large round rings.

The Unit A beads are strung on the 24 gauge silver wire. Remember when using 24 gauge wire you need to bend the wire at a right angle leaving about an inch of wire. Wind around the round nose pliers in 2 turns to make then circle and the wrap the rest of the wire around the wire about 4 times. Cut off the excess. Make sure the cut is a sharp, clean cut and if necessary file the edge so there are no sharp edges.

Earrings

Make 2 Unit As, 2 Unit Ds, and 2 Unit Cs. Attach a Unit D which is strung on a T-pin to Unit A with a large round ring, then attach the two pieces to the earring finding, with a large round ring. Unit C is also strung on a T-pin and attached to the earring finding with 3 large rings.

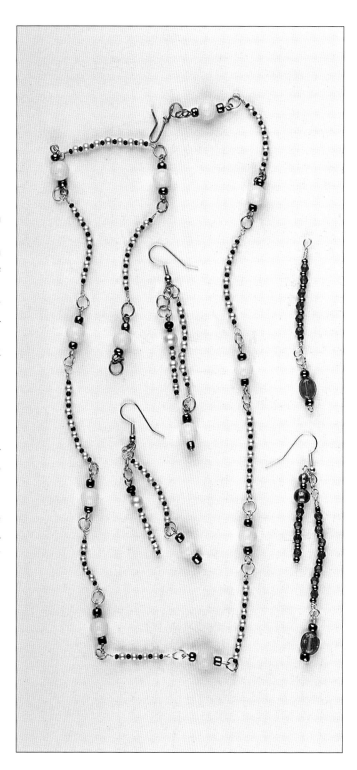

Long and Lean

This title is how I wish my body was; what I wouldn't give for legs that go on forever. This necklace is longer than most, at about 21 inches. What started the design for me were the tiny pink and white beads that look like tiger eyes. "How can I use them in a necklace?," I asked myself.

Materials:
24 gauge gold-filled wire (because the opening in the bead
    I love is very small)
20 gauge gold wire
 3 flat green beads
18 small green beads
24 small flat beads (black, brown and green)
34 small pink and white tiger eye beads

String the green flat beads on 20 gauge wire. All the other units are strung on 24 gauge wire and closed with the loop and wrap method. Each unit is connected by a single 20 gauge wire ring, and the last unit has 3 rings before the clasp is attached.

The center is a single green bead.

Two units of 3 green beads are separated by 2 tiger eye beads separates three single green beads.

A double strand of 2 tiger eyes and 4 small flat beads, followed by a single unit of 3 green beads, separated by 2 tiger eye beads repeated 2 times, and then ends with a double string of 2 tiger eyes, and 4 small flat beads.

Brown All The Way

This design is exceptionally long, which means it looks well on collarless sweaters or under the collar of a blouse. The different sizes of the beads, along with the different style beads, make this an interesting necklace. It is a great design to use leftover beads.

Materials:

20 gauge gold wire
2   large brown translucent beads
6   medium size brown beads with a painted flower design
6   oblong light brown translucent beads
7   small barrel brass metal beads
2   tiger eye brown beads
2   curved flat bronze disc beads
10 large copper flowers
4   small copper flowers
4   medium size copper metal beads
24 small bronze, metal beads
8   wood gold beads
4   small oblong raised gold bead

Unit A- small bronze metal bead, small barrel brass metal bead, small bronze metal bead
Unit B- wood gold bead, oblong light brown translucent bead, wood gold bead
Unit C- small oblong raised gold bead, brown bead with painted flower design, small oblong raised gold bead
Unit D- large copper flower, large brown translucent bead, large copper flower
Unit E - large copper flower, brown bead with painted flower design, large copper flower
Unit F- small bronze metal bead, small barrel brass metal bead, small bronze metal bead
Unit G- small bronze metal bead, large copper flower, small bronze meal bead
Unit H- small bronze metal bead, curved flat bronze disc bead, medium size copper metal bead, tiger eye bead, medium copper metal bead
Unit I- small gold bead, small bronze metal bead, flower brown bead, small bronze metal bead and small gold bead

That is some variety. Interesting to do, it was easy to put together.
In the center is Unit A.

For one side attach with figure eights throughout Unit B, Unit C, Unit D, Unit A, Unit E, Unit A, Unit G, Unit B, Unit I, Unit B, Unit A. Repeat the same attachment for the other side.

The earrings are one unit on a T pin attached to the earring finding with a medium size gold ring. Use Unit H.

🌸 *11. Pendants* 🌸

Silver Wrapped Turquoise

Left

Materials:
20 gauge sterling silver wire
5 wrapped turquoise beads
28 assorted sizes of turquoise beads
8 medium size silver balls
4 sterling silver tubes

This is easy to make. The beads were bought wrapped, but are not difficult to make with 24 gauge or thinner wire. Each unit is filled with a variety of turquoise beads. The front units are shorter. The unit with the silver tube starts with a medium silver ball, silver tube and then a medium silver ball. Make 4 silver tube units and 8 units of assorted beads.

Leave some beads for the pendant. That hangs from the center bead, which is a wrapped bead. On a T-pin, string a small oval bead, larger irregular shaped bead, and a medium size deep turquoise metal bead. Attach the T-pin to the wrapped bead with 2 rings. Attach 2 more rings and then 4 rings, so that 2 go to each side.

The sequence of the chain is 2 ring flower, which means the rings are interlocked, single ring, single ring, 2 ring flower, single ring, 2 ring flower, single ring, 2 ring flower , single ring,2 ring flower, single ring , single ring and single ring.

The sequence of the beads is Short unit, Silver tube unit, wrapped bead, medium unit, wrapped bead, medium unit, silver tube unit and medium unit.

Blue Medallion

Right

In a local bead store, the blue medallion was a favorite of my husband. He loves the color blue and I thought the shape was very attractive. I found the round flower beads that I really liked. I combined the new medallion and round flower beads with complimentary small oval beads iridescent blue, and small yellow beads along with turquoise beads that I already had.

After finishing the necklace I bought a blouse to compliment my new jewelry. This sounds ridiculous to some and totally on course to others.

Materials:
20 gauge sterling silver wire
8 large blue and yellow flower beads
28 small turquoise beads
6 small yellow beads
20 small blue iridescent oval beads
2 irregular shaped turquoise beads
4 medium turquoise beads
4 silver beads
4 darker blue rectangular beads

Make 6 units of the flower bead surrounded by the blue iridescent oval beads and small turquoise beads.

These are combined with 3 units using yellow beads.

The following units go *between* the flower bead units. Each unit is different.

The units start with dark blue rectangular beads surrounding a yellow bead, followed by a yellow bead surrounded by iridescent blue oval beads,

and ends with a yellow bead surrounded by medium turquoise beads and silver beads.

Earrings
The earrings have a flower unit that is the same as the necklace, with a small irregular-shaped turquoise bead, surrounded by 2 small turquoise beads strung on a T-pin.

The connector is a 3-group chain and a round ring.

The flower unit is connected to the earring holder with a double set of rings.

The medallion is on a double set of medium rings followed by 2 more sets of medium rings with a total of 3 sets of 2 medium rings, before the two sides are connected with a single ring on each side.

Sometimes you see something and just know that it would be fun to work with. The center green bead caught my attention and my husband suggested that I do beading with the big bead.

Materials:
20 gauge sterling silver wire
Assorted seed beads –black, pink, white
and green in varying sizes
9 brown and green speckled tear drops
19 small dark green beads
5   silver beads
21 small green beads
20 oval green beads
20   small pearl beads
4   small white beads
4   silver engraved beads
28 metal green beds

2 iridescent green beads
4 head pins
2 earring findings
1 extra long head pin

Center Bead- Glue the bead to a piece of leather. Sew beads one at a time through the leather and around the bead. Glue a piece of black felt to the leather so that he sewing doesn't show.

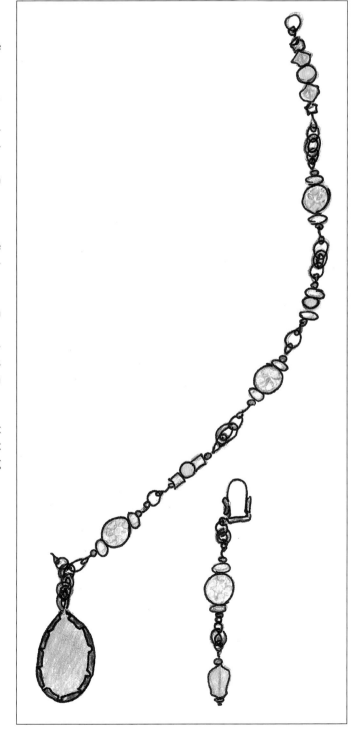

❧ 12. Unusual Beads ❧

From Speckled to Barney Rubble

My taste is certainly eclectic. We start with a green and red speckled clear bead and end with a gold confetti speckled gold bead. In between is black, iridescent and gold in its glory and the best of the bunch is my "Barney Rubble" necklace, which you who are old enough to remember "The Flintstones" can relate to.

Left

Materials:
20 gauge sterling silver wire
10 green and red speckled beads
6 very light green beads
2 gold raised circle beads
8 speckled green beads
28 seed bead size red and green metal beads
10 pink (4), green (6) small beads
4 silver beads

The green and red beads are strung with a combination of other beads.

Unit A- Seed bead green, small green bead, green/red bead, green bead, seed bead green. Make 2.
Unit B- Seed bead green, red/green, seed bead green. Make 4.
Unit C- Seed bead green, pink, red/green, pink, seed bead green. Make 2.
The light green beads are also strung with a combination of other beads.
Unit D- Seed bead red, gold raise circle, light green gold raised circle, seed bead red. Make 2.
Unit E- Silver, speckled green, very light green, speckled green, silver Make 2.
Unit F- Seed bead red, speckled green, Very Light green, speckled green, speckled green, seed bead red. Make 2.

All the units are connected with a medium size ring.
I strung them with 2 of the red/green bead combinations and then a very light green bead combination. The order otherwise doesn't really matter, so combine however you want.

Center

Materials:
20 gauge gold wire
8 oblong very dark greenish black beads
16 small metal black and green beads
16 small gold beads
9 short gold tube

Surround the oblong dark greenish black beads with a gold bead, small metal black or green bead on both sides. String the short gold tube alone. Combine the pieces by alternating the very dark greenish black bead with the short gold tube. And connect with medium size gold rings.

Right

Materials:
20 gauge copper wire
8 large iridescent green, purple, red stones
4 large metal oval bluish purple beads
2 red metal barrels
1 large translucent purple bead
30 small metal red, and green beads

String each of the different kinds of beads with a small metal red or green bead to start and at the finish giving you 3 beads to each unit. The large purple bead is in then center. Between each of the large iridescent green, purple, red stones place the metal oval bluish purple beads and the red metal barrels right before the last bead. Connect with medium size copper rings.

Left

Materials:
20 gauge silver wire
6 small silver balls
6 short silver tubes
12 Raised round 3 tier silver ball
1 medium size lined silver ball
2 silver ball caps
6 small raised tier ball
24 speckled green ovals
8 oval speckled confetti beads
2 flat oval translucent beads
2 earring findings
4 medium size lined silver balls
4 small size lined silver balls.
2 silver hearts

Unit A, Center- small raised tier ball, bead cap, medium size lined silver ball, bead cap, small raised tier ball. Make 1.
Unit B- 3 tier silver ball, speckled green oval, oval speckled confetti bead, speckled green oval, small raised tier ball. Make 6
Unit C- speckled green oval, oval speckled confetti bead, speckled green oval. Make 2
Unit D- speckled green oval, flat translucent bead, speckled green oval. Make 2
Unit E- silver ball, short silver tube twice and ending with a silver ball. Make 2.

Attach with medium size rings with A in the center, Unit B, Unit C, Unit B, Unit D, Unit B, and end with Unit E. Repeat in reverse for the other side.

Earrings
Hang a heart from a small lined ball, medium lined ball, small lined ball unit, attached to a handmade finding with a medium lined silver ball.

Center

Materials:
20 gauge gold wire
7 very dark greenish black small round beads
8 long gold tubes
14 small gold beads
24 gauge silver wire

String the long gold tubes alone. String the small greenish black round beads surrounded by the small gold beads. Use the 24 gauge wire for 3 and the 20 gauge gold wire for 4. Alternate a gold tube with a round bead ending with the gold tube. There are 15 units in all.

Right

Materials:
20 gauge silver wire
An assortment of sizes and shapes in metallic, iridescent, green, red and purple beads:
8 raised double pyramids
8 medium size faceted black beads
6 round iridescent beads
6 small size faceted black/green beads
8 small metal barrels
1 large round metal bead
14 seed bead size metal beads
4 flat tubes in iridescent green/purple.

Unit A- small faceted bead, small metal barrel, large round bead, metal barrel, faceted bead. This is the center.
Unit B- seed bead, pyramid, barrel, round, barrel. Make 2
Unit C- sm. Faceted black/green, pyramid, faceted. Make 2
Unit D- barrel, med. Faceted black, barrel. Make 2
Unit E- med. black faceted, Pyramid, med. Black faceted. Make 4
Unit F- sm. Seed bead twice, barrel, Round iridescent bead, barrel, seed bead twice. Make 2
Unit G- flat tube, seed bead, round iridescent, seed bead, flat tube. Make 2

String on each side as follows: B, C, D, E, F, E, and G. Attach all with medium-size silver rings.

87

Unusual Beads

Sometimes we come across unusual beads and if we like them our job as jewelry designers is to find a way to use the beads in a wearable design. The translucent cross bar with 2 holes was a gift from a fellow teacher who was cleaning out her mother's craft materials. She knew I made jewelry so I got a stash of a lot of different items. The purple beads came from a necklace that was actually given to me as a gift, which I proceeded to take apart because it was a chocker necklace and I can't stand anything tight around my neck.

Materials:
20 gauge silver wire
23 purple dog bone beads with 2 holes
80 small purple beads
Jig #28

Unit A- 2 dog bone beads separated by purple beads and beginning and ending with purple beads
Unit B- 1 dog bone bead surrounded by 2 purple beads on each side.
Unit C- 2 purple beads followed by a dog bone bead through only one hole and then 2 purple beads The wire is curved after the beads are strung.

String Unit C as the center followed by Unit B 2 times and then a jig piece, Unit B 2 times, Unit A, and a jig piece, Unit B, and then a jig piece, and Unit A twice.

There are 8 units on each side of the necklace. All the units are connected by small rings.

Combinations

Unique combinations of beads that compliment each other in both size and color and are separated by silver and gold two ring chains.

See Page 93

Green with Chips and a Touch of Pink

Far left

Materials:
20 gauge silver wire
20 gauge silver wire
32 green speckled teardrops
37 gold wood small beads
22 small pinkish purple translucent beads

Unit A- gold, drop green, gold, drop green, pink, drop green, gold, drop green, gold. Make 4.
Unit B- gold, pink, green, gold, pink, green, gold, pink, green, gold. Make 2.
Unit C- gold, green, pink, gold, green, pink, gold, green, pink, gold, green, pink, gold, green, pink, gold, green, pink, gold. Make 2.

Put 4 Unit As in the front connected to each other. Follow with a Unit B and a Unit C on each side.

The connecting chain is 6 double rings of silver and gold connected in 3s, and joined in the center by a single ring of either gold or silver. Make 3.

The next connectors are 5 double rings connected together and attached to the units with a single gold or silver ring. Make 2.

The last connectors are 4 double rings of silver and gold connected in 2s and joined in the center by a single ring of either silver or gold. Make 2.

Single Cloisonné Center and Double Chain

Delicate, double chained and coordinated for a wonderfully alive and light necklace.

Left of Center

Materials:
1 cloisonné bead medium size
64 seed bead size green beads
64 seed bead size pink beads
64 seed bead size purple beads
170 seed bead size pink/ white tiger eye beads
24 gauge gold wire.
20 gauge gold wire.

Unit A- tiger eye, green, tiger eye, green, Cloisonné, tiger eye, green, tiger eye.
Unit B- tiger eye, tiger eye, purple green, pink, tiger eye, tiger eye, purple, green, pink, tiger eye, tiger eye, purple, green, pink, tiger eye, tiger eye . Make 16 units and break into 4 units of 2 each.
Unit C- tiger eye, tiger eye, purple, green, pink, tiger eye, tiger eye, purple, green, pink, tiger eye, tiger eye, purple, green, pink, tiger eye, tiger eye. Make 4 units and break into 2 units of 2 each.
Unit D- Make a single chain of unit C. Make 2.

Connect the units with a medium size gold ring. Attach 2 units to each of the gold rings until the last unit, which is single.

Double Ring Copper and Turquoise

A long, very turquoise with large ring connectors and simple to make

Center

Materials:
20 gauge copper wire
32 medium size turquoise beads
1   bright metallic turquoise bead
1   translucent light green heart
66 small light blue translucent beads
6   seed bead size black beads

Make 2 large rings with 4 blue beads on each ring. When attaching a unit to the ring make sure that 2 blue beads are on each side of the attachment.

Unit A- blue bead, turquoise bead, black bead, turquoise bead, blue bead on a T pin. Make 2.
Unit B- blue bead, turquoise bead, blue bead, heart, black bead, blue bead on a T pin.
Attach Unit B to the ring with 2 blue beads on each side.
Attach the Unit As to the same ring with one unit on each side and between the 2 blue beads that are on each side of the unit a attachment.
Unit C- blue bead, bright metallic turquoise bead, blue bead on a T- pin.
Attach Unit B to the second ring that has 4 blue beads between the beads and having two on each side.
Unit D- blue bead, turquoise bead, black bead, turquoise bead, blue bead on a T-pin. Make 2.
These are attached to the end of 2 of the rest of the units.
Unit E- blue bead, turquoise bead, blue bead. String on 20 gauge copper wire. Make 22.

String the 22 units with 11 on each, alternate, connecting with a large copper ring and a small copper ring. Remember to attach Unit D to the end of the first 2 units that are connected to the ring with 4 beads.

Double Strung Silver and Light Green

Right of Center

Materials
20 gauge silver wire
1   large light green oblong shaped bead
22 light blue clear beads
46 speckle green discs
12 silver discs
8   short light green tube beads
12 small light black beads
8   small silver beads

Unit A- The center is a green disc, blue bead, large green oblong bead, blue bead, green disc. Make 1.
All units are attached with a medium size silver ring. Attached to the center unit are two strands of beads on each side.
Unit B, Strand 1- green disc, silver bead, silver disc, blue, silver disc, silver bead, green disc.
Unit B, Strand 2- black bead, green disc, green tube, green disc, black bead. These 3 strands are attached with a single ring to one side of the center after being attached to each other.
Unit B, Strand 3- green disc, blue bead, green disc, black bead, green disc, blue bead, green disc.
Unit C, Strand 1- blue bead, green tune, blue bead.
Unit C, Strand 2- green disc, silver bead, silver disc, blue bead, silver disc, silver bead, green disc.
Unit C, Strand 3- black bead, green disc, green tube, green disc, black bead.

After attaching to each other, attach to the same side of the center as Unit B.

Make identical strands for the other side. You should have made in all 12 different units with 3 strands attached for each supper unit and 4 supper units that are split and attached with 2 to one side and 2 to the other side. Make sure that you finished with the right amount of units.

Outside attachment is made with 2 single medium size rings on the bottom and 2 single medium size rings on the top.

Inside attachment is made with hooking into the first ring of the outside attachment on the bottom and the last ring of the outside attachment on the top. The other side is attached the same way.

Unit D- green disc, blue bead, green disc, silver bead, green disc, blue bead, green disc. Make 2

Unit E- green disc, blue bead, silver disc, blue bead, silver bead, silver disc, blue bead, silver bead and green disc. Make 2

Unit F- blue bead, green disc, green tube, green disc, blue bead. Make 2.

Unit G- green disc, silver bead, silver disc, blue bead, silver disc, silver bead, green disc. Make 2.

Attach Units D, E, F and G on each side, with medium-sized silver rings.

Beige, White and Silver-Understated

Far Right

Materials:
27 white and beige small beads
20 gauge silver wire
8 silver discs
14 antique gold small discs
16 very small silver beads
36 small silver beads.
2 earring findings
4 short T-pins

Unit A- small silver bead, beige/white bead, small silver bead. Make 16.

Unit B- gold disc, beige/white bead, gold disc. Make 7.

Unit C- small silver bead, silver disc, white/beige bead, silver disc, small silver bead. Make 4.

The necklace attachments with a medium size silver ring are a Unit B in the center, and on each side Unit C, Unit A, Unit A, Unit B, Unit C, Unit A, Unit B, Unit A, Unit A, Unit A.

Earrings

Earrings have 4 components. On a T-pin are a very small silver bead, small silver bead, very small silver bead. Make 4, 2 for each earring.

With a medium size ring, attach a Unit A to each of the T-Pin units.

With a medium size silver ring attach a Unit B, which is the attached to the earring finding with another medium size silver ring.

Two is Better Than One

Sometimes two is better than one. I often wear two necklaces together.

Outside

Materials:
20 gauge gold wire
20 gauge copper wire
5   disc light green beads
22 seed bead size lt. green beads
10 oval lt. green beads
10 gold lined short tube
10 black metal bead
2   flat gold discs
16 assorted colors (lt. blue, green, pink) of sm. Glass beads
36 assorted sm. Seed bead size beads (copper, gold, silver,)

Unit A- seed bead, gold tube, black metal bead, flat gold disc, green disc, gold disc, black metal bead, gold tube, seed bead. Make 5.
Unit B- seed bead assorted, seed bead lt. green, glass bead, 2 seed bead assorted, lt. green oval bead, seed bead, glass bead, seed bead. Make 10.
In these 10 units there is some variation in the arrangement of beads, but the length is consistently the same.

The connectors for the units are a medium size ring, flower rings, and a medium size ring.

To make the flower ring, put two rings together and add a third ring to the unit. Remember to have the rings overlapping in the same way each time, and laying flat when the 3 rings are connected. It is easy to do and adds an interesting element.

Inside

Materials:
20 gauge gold wire
20 gauge copper wire
1   large lt. green bead
9   med size round lt. green beads
14 gold lined short tube
34 assorted glass beads
12 assorted seed beads
17 metal black beads
12 speckled green tear drops

There are 12 units of equal length and a center unit of approximately the same length. Use the assortment of beads and create your own units. I did make 2 of each unit I created so that the sides would be the same. Connect with medium ring.

 Supplies

Here are some jewelry-making supply stores that have been a good source for me in my local area, Nassau County, New York, and elsewhere, and some on-line supply sites. The internet has a vast amount of sites that will lead the user to jewelry supply places by typing in "jewelry supplies." Happy jewelry making!

Ace Handcraft
314 Hempstead Turnpike, New York 11552
1-516-292-1478

Michaels
3610 Long Beach Road, Oceanside, New York 11572
1-516-855-0220

Pearl Art and Craft
2000 Hempstead Turnpike, East Meadow, New York 11554
1-516-542-7700

A.C.Moore
Clock tower Place 157 Glen Cove Road, New York, 11514
1-516-294-8401

Beads and Things
539 Bedford Avenue, Bellmore, New York
1-516-783-1124

Nice People Inc.
P.O. Box 661 Rhinebeck, New York 12572
1-845-876-8802 (they travel and do shows at various places to sell their supplies)

Fire Mountain Gems and Beads
One Fire Mountain Way Grants Pass, Oregon 97326-2373 USA
1-800-355-2137
www.firemountaingem.com

Oriental Trading Company
P.O. Box 2308 Omaha, Nebraska. 68103-2308
1-800-228-2269
www.orientaltrading.com

Magazines

Bead Style
P.O.Box 1612
Waukesha WI, 5317-1612
1-800-533-6644

Bead and Button
Kalmbach Publishing Co.
21027 Cross Roads Circle
P.O.Box 1612
Waukesha Wi, 53187-1612
akorach@beadandbutton.com

Beadwork
Interweave Press Inc.
201 East 4th Street
Loveland, Colorado 80537
1-970-669-7672
www.interweave.com
Beadwork@pcspublink.com
1-800-849-8753
P.O.Box 469105, Escondido, California 92046-9105

References

Clegg, Helen, and Mary Larom, *Making Wire Jewelry*, Asheville, North Carolina: Lark Books, 1997.

Cusick, Dawn, *Making Bead and Wire jewelry*, Asheville, North Carolina: Lark Books, 2000.

Peterson, Irene, *Great Wire Jewelry*, Asheville, North Carolina: Lark Books, 1998.

Springtzen, Alice, *The Jeweler's Art*, Worcester, Massachusetts: Davis Publications, 1995.